100INDIEROCK RIFFSFORGUITAR

Learn 100 Indie Rock Guitar Riffs in the Style of the World's 20 Greatest Players

JOSEPH**ALEXANDER**
& PETE**SKLAROFF**

FUNDAMENTAL**CHANGES**

100 Indie Rock Riffs for Guitar

Learn 100 Indie Rock Guitar Riffs in the Style of the World's 20 Greatest Players

ISBN: 978-1-78933-034-2

Published by www.fundamental-changes.com

www.fundamental-changes.com

Twitter: **@guitar_joseph**

Over 10,000 fans on Facebook: **FundamentalChangesInGuitar**

Instagram: **FundamentalChanges**

For over 350 Free Guitar Lessons with Videos Check Out

www.fundamental-changes.com

Cover Image Copyright: Shutterstock - Roman Voloshyn

Contents

Introduction

"In the Style of…" What does that mean?

To write this book we immersed ourselves in the music of each of the artists covered and spent hours listening to hundreds of tracks. While these one hundred licks are not transcribed directly from the records, they are as stylistically accurate as we can make them.

Each of the five licks for every artist is designed to encapsulate their approach to soloing in a couple of bars. For example, a Johnny Marr example in this book should make you say "Ahhh! That's Johnny alright!"

Of course, it's impossible to encapsulate the style of a player in just five phrases – the musicians featured here are all talented, complex individuals with rich musical vocabularies; a whole book could be devoted to each one (maybe one day we'll do that)!

Rather, the phrases here are intended as a starting point for your exploration of each guitarist and their music. If you work through all the examples in this book and practise the licks so that you absorb them into your playing, you'll build a comprehensive **Indie** vocabulary and be well on your way to developing your own style.

You may have bought this book as a shortcut to writing Indie-style guitar riffs and songs. We are confident it will help you, especially with the stylistic aspects of each player. Most rock vocabulary is chord, texture, or riff based, but the way that each guitarist makes phrases personal and unique to them is probably the biggest insight this book can give you.

We all expand our vocabulary by copying phrases from other people – it's how language works. So the best practice you can do to take your playing further is to transcribe the solos of your favourite artists. Turn off the cell phone, close Facebook and just sit with your guitar, figuring out the licks you love. Cherry pick the textures that jump out at you and master them, note by note. That way you'll expand your vocabulary in the style you love and, above all, you'll sound like *you*.

Finally, please download the audio for the book. Reading music off paper is one thing, but you really need to hear each lick to get a feel for how it's played. Music is all about feel. While the notation will show you the notes, the audio will give you the all-important phrasing and nuance. Instructions for getting the audio for free are on the next page.

Above all, have fun exploring the music of these incredible modern Indie Rock guitarists. Apply everything musically and focus on learning what you enjoy hearing.

We had a huge amount of fun putting this book together. We hope it's equally as enjoyable to learn from and provides a unique insight into the music of the guitarists you love.

Good Luck!

Joseph and Pete

N.B. While we have made these riffs and ideas as stylistically accurate as possible, no transcription has taken place and every example is original. The names of artists in this book are provided as a musical reference only, and Fundamental Changes Ltd. are in no way associated with the artists mentioned.

Get the Audio

The audio files for this book are available to download for free from **www.fundamental-changes.com.** The link is in the top right-hand corner. Simply select this book title from the drop-down menu and follow the instructions to get the audio.

We recommend that you download the files directly to your computer, not to your tablet, and extract them there before adding them to your media library. You can then put them on your tablet, iPod or burn them to CD. On the download page there is a help PDF and we also provide technical support via the contact form.

www.fundamental-changes.com

Kindles / eReaders

To get the most out of this book, remember that you can double tap any image to enlarge it. Turn off 'column viewing' and hold your kindle in landscape mode.

Over 10,000 fans on Facebook: FundamentalChangesInGuitar

Get featured on Instagram: @FundamentalChanges

For over 350 Free Guitar Lessons with Videos Check Out

www.fundamental-changes.com

Robert Smith (The Cure)

Robert James Smith was born in Blackpool, England on 21st April 1959. His unique writing/guitar style and equally distinctive stage image had a profound effect upon the Goth musical culture in the early 1980s. He founded the group The Cure in West Sussex, England, in 1976 and worked as the lead guitarist for Siouxsie and the Banshees for a brief period in the early 1980s.

Smith began playing the guitar at the age of 9 when he started classical guitar lessons and by his early teens had moved onto the electric guitar. While still at school, he began forming bands with his classmates and after playing with several different groups, he eventually co-founded The Cure, who released their first album *Three Imaginary Boys* in 1979.

Firmly based in the Post-Punk and New Wave music of the day, the group initially produced recordings that were dark, introspective and moody. As a result, they became favourites within the emerging gothic rock movement, although Smith now prefers to distance himself from this association.

By the early-mid 1980s, Smith began to move away from his sombre compositional style and sought to introduce more of a mainstream pop element to his songs. The Cure later had notable commercial success with singles like *Just Like Heaven, Lovesong* and *Friday I'm in Love*.

Since the 1980s, The Cure have gone through numerous line-up changes, but Robert Smith has remained as the creative guiding force of the group and its only consistent member. In more recent years, and despite fluctuating sales and some lacklustre recordings, the group have continued to write and tour. It is rumoured that a new studio recording may be produced in 2019 to mark the 40th anniversary of their first recording.

Guitar style, instruments and equipment

Smith's instrumental approach is very much dependent upon the individual song he is playing. For example, he often detunes the instrument to create specific tones and sonic effects in the studio. He also employs diverse stylistic approaches in his playing, ranging from Middle Eastern sounding guitar melodies through to extended soloing such as heard on tracks like *A Forest*. Acoustic guitars feature in many of his recordings as well as more typical distorted rock guitar tones and feedback effects.

Smith began his career with The Cure by using a cheap Woolworth's Top 20 guitar, which was later replaced by a Fender Jazzmaster (incidentally a popular choice with many Indie Rock guitarists). He has also used classical and acoustic guitars as well as a distinctive sounding Fender VI (a six-string electric bass guitar) on Cure recordings. Other instruments include guitars by Epiphone, Gretsch and Schecter. He has also had several custom-built guitars made for him including the Schecter RS Ultracure model.

For amplifiers, he has variously used a Roland Jazz Chorus, a Vox AC30 and a Marshall Bluesbreaker combo. A keen advocate of effects units, he employs a variety of Roland Boss pedals and Line 6 units, covering popular effects such as chorusing, flanging, wah-wah, delay and reverb.

Recommended Listening

The Cure – *Three Imaginary Boys*

The Cure – *Disintegration*

The Cure – *Pornography*

The Cure – *Faith*

Using the open E string as a drone, Example 1a is a simple sounding melody figure that progressively adjusts to match the underlying harmony of the song. In bar one, a slide from the 3rd fret on the B string up to the 5th fret leads to a doubling of the open E string. This technique is then developed throughout the remainder of the example with the notes on the B string being used to highlight different chord tones.

Many Indie Rock guitar players use this approach to create compelling rhythm guitar parts or counter-melodies and the technique has its roots in acoustic blues guitar, where a very similar approach is used. Make sure you keep the rhythms accurate to match the backing track and let the notes in each bar ring against each other.

Example 1a

Example 1b

This example uses a mixture of major and minor triads and four/five note chord structures. There's nothing rhythmically complex here, as you simply sustain each chord for the first three beats of every bar. The first four bars use triads exclusively and note that these are all played on the D, G and B strings. Keeping triads on the same string set can help a rhythm guitar part remain consistent tonally (a secret many recording guitarists know well).

Four and five note voicings are used in the second part of this example to thicken up the sound a little and notice that some tremolo effect has been added to the guitar sound to create a shimmering effect. The use of a tremolo effect on clean guitar sounds is very common in Indie Rock music.

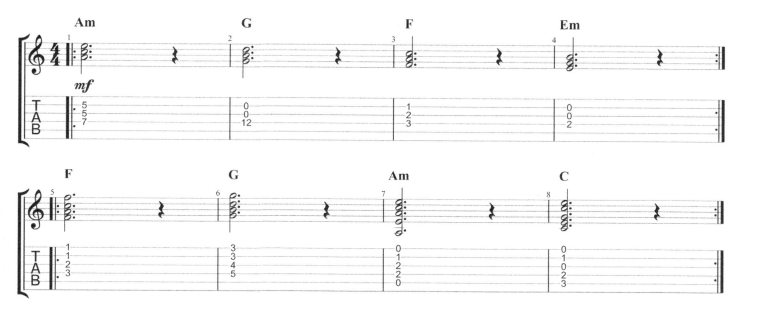

The use of repeated 1/8th note rhythms in Indie Rock music is commonplace and they are either played with a clean tone (as seen here) or with a distorted guitar sound. The rhythm is constant throughout this lick, but the notes change to outline the harmony of the song and make for an effective melody line as a result. Many funk guitarists use this approach as well.

Keeping consistent time is crucial with this type of rhythm guitar part. Listen carefully to the drums to ensure that you are locked-in with them. Some palm-muting is employed here as well to add a percussive effect. Note that this muting is eventually released towards the final bar to create a short crescendo rising to the F major chord in the final bar.

Example 1c

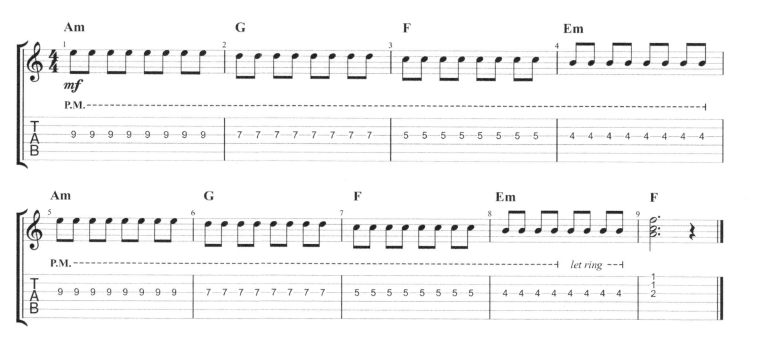

This next example is a single line and double-stop lick and is based around an A minor pentatonic scale. It would work well as a counter melody to a lead vocal and uses some small string bends (as seen in bars two and six). The lick begins in the 8th position on the fingerboard and then moves quickly to a familiar pentatonic 'box' position located around the fifth fret region.

The final two bars utilise the open (top) E string and you'll need to move your hand down to third position to accommodate the slide at the beginning of bar eight. Remember to add a little vibrato as indicated in bars one and five.

Example 1d

The final Robert Smith lick uses both open position and barre chords and shows how simple chord forms can work very effectively within a rhythm guitar track. Each chord is held for a total of three beats and is played with a distinctive strum going from the lowest note of the chord to the highest. You will have to start your chord strum slightly early (just before the downbeat of each bar) to make sure the chord falls in time with the backing track.

The guitar tone here is very much influenced by 1960s recordings with a noticeable treble boost and some vibrato added to the sound. If you are able to, try to set your vibrato effect to be in time with the track tempo.

Example 1e

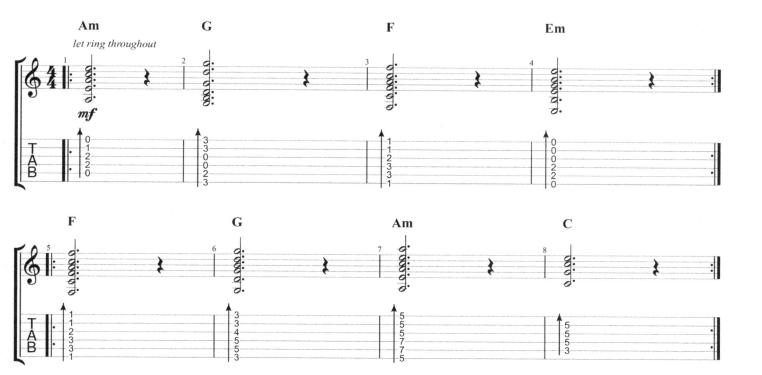

Will Sergeant (Echo and the Bunnymen)

William Alfred Sergeant was born in Liverpool, England, on 12th April 1958. He is best known as the guitarist for the group Echo and the Bunnymen who also began their performing and recording career in Liverpool. Sergeant was initially inspired by punk rock and the raw approach taken by late 70s New Wave bands from England, but was equally influenced by late 60s US rock, particularly the psychedelic movement represented by bands such as the Velvet Underground and The Doors.

Sergeant formed the group Echo and the Bunnymen with singer Ian McCulloch and bassist Les Pattinson in 1978 and they released their first album *Crocodiles* in 1980. At this stage, the group (unusually) did not use a drummer and relied on a drum machine instead. They later added a live drummer to the group's line-up and had some initial commercial success with this first recording which quickly entered the top 20 of the UK album charts.

A second album called *Heaven Up Here* was released the following year which cemented their initial success and the single *The Cutter* (from the album *Porcupine*) saw the band attain a Top 10 single. Subsequent singles continued the band's commercial growth which continued until McCulloch left in 1988, leaving the future of the group in the balance. The drummer of the group (Pete de Freitas) was tragically killed in a motorcycle accident, further adding to the uncertainty of their future.

The group elected to continue working and added a new singer and drummer to the band. This line-up recorded their next album *Reverberation*, but it was not especially well received by the group's fan base and they disbanded completely in 1993. Sergeant and McCulloch then decided to work together again in 1994 under the name *Electrafixation* before adding Les Pattinson back into the fold and resurrecting the band's original name once more. The original members then recorded the album *Evergreen* in 1997.

The group has continued to record and perform ever since and has steadily released new recordings throughout the 2000s. Their most recent record, *Meteorites,* was released in 2014 – the band's first top 40 album since the late 1990s.

Guitar style, instruments and equipment

Will Sergeant's guitar work is a central feature of Echo and the Bunnymen. He employs a lot of reverb and delay on his guitar tone and his playing has influenced many other players of the Indie Rock movement.

Sergeant's main guitar in the 1980s was a black Fender Telecaster and occasionally a Fender Jaguar or Stratocaster. He has also periodically recorded with a Vox 12 string guitar.

For amplification, Sergeant has used Laney and Fender amplifiers along with other models such as the Roland Jazz Chorus. His effects units include models made by Blackstar, Roland (Boss GT-8) and Maxon to help him achieve his distinctive cutting guitar tones. He has also used an E-Bow sustain unit.

Recommended Listening

Echo and the Bunnymen – *Ocean Rain*

Echo and the Bunnymen – *Heaven Up Here*

Echo and the Bunnymen – *Porcupine*

Echo and the Bunnymen – *Crocodiles*

Using an echo and reverb laden guitar tone very typical of Will Sergeant, this example demonstrates just how effective a simple riff can be when played with a distinctive sound. The riff itself is constructed from a melodic motif outlining the 4th, 3rd and root/octave of a B7 chord. Nothing technically demanding here, but make sure you follow the rhythm exactly as written, referring to the audio as required.

This lick is what is sometimes referred to as a 'question and answer' style riff, with the first 'question' phrase in bar one being answered by the second phrase beginning in bar three. You may need to set the level of your delay and reverb effects a bit higher than normal here too.

Example 2a

This combined 1/8th and 1/16th note lick could easily be heard in a funk or RnB song, but works very effectively here as a strong rhythmic guitar part. It also uses the two bar 'question and answer' approach seen in the last example. Employ plenty of palm-muting to achieve the 'clicking' effect heard on the recording and pay particular attention to locking in with the backing track rhythm and tempo.

The entire lick is played around the 7th fret region of the fingerboard and highlights chord tones from the B7 chord (specifically the Root, b7, 3rd and 4th). You may need to pick a little harder than normal to get the sound heard on the recording.

Example 2b

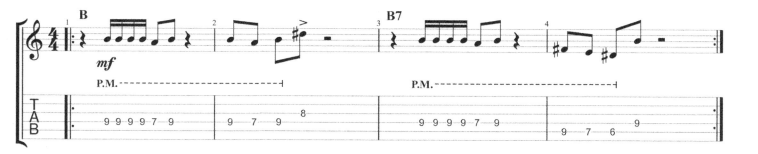

This next lick is considerably enhanced by the guitar tone, which uses a very compressed clean guitar signal, some delay and plenty of reverb. Beginning in bar one, a B major triad is played with the tremolo arm to create a subtle vibrato. In bars three and four, the same triad is used again and this time is played by slightly 'dipping' the tremolo arm in advance of the downbeat before bringing it up to pitch.

After the repeat of the first four bars, a tremolo arm approach is used with the single note in bar five and then the two-note interval figure following it. Single or two note figures like this can be very effective in a rhythm guitar part, especially if the guitar tone stands out within the track. The final four bars utilise four note major chords to thicken out the sound a little.

Example 2c

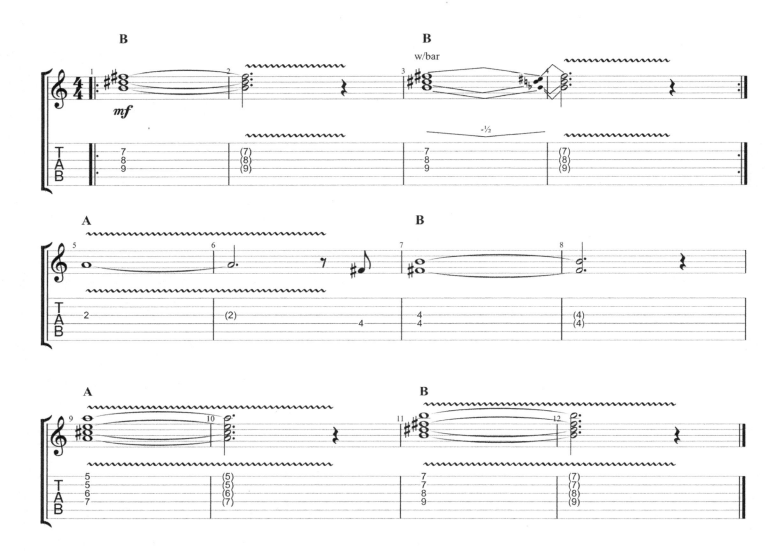

The melody in this lick sounds almost Middle Eastern in nature and is constructed from a dominant 11th arpeggio. A dominant 11th arpeggio is a regular dominant 7th arpeggio with an added 4th/11th degree. The lick is divided into two-bar sections and would make a good counter melody to a vocal line or even a short instrumental break within a song.

You can play the lick entirely within the 7th position on the fingerboard. Watch the offbeat 1/8th note rhythm at the beginning of each two-bar phrase, where you will begin each phrase on the '&' (offbeat) of beat one. Add some reverb and a short delay to get closer to the Will Sergeant sound.

Example 2d

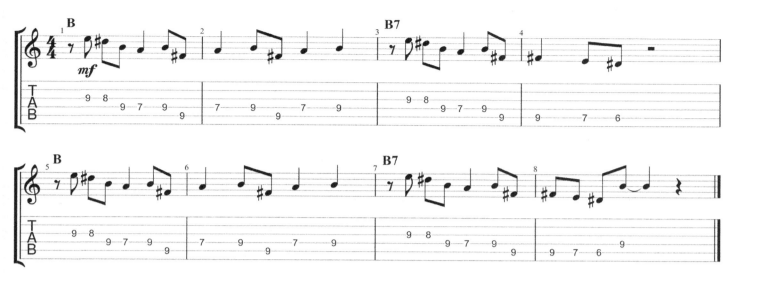

This lick could easily have come from a 1970s Jeff Beck or Pink Floyd album, as it uses a lot of double-stops, triads and finger vibrato typical of that era. The lick is mostly played in the 6th and 7th positions on the fingerboard and although technically quite straightforward to play, you may need to refer to the audio to get the exact rhythms. Watch out for the 1/4 note triplets in bar two especially. In bar ten, remember to play the slide indicated on the third string between the 6th and 8th frets.

Try to let the indicated notes ring for as long as possible and use an overdriven guitar tone, again with some reverb and delay added.

Example 2e

Peter Buck (R.E.M.)

Peter Lawrence Buck was born in Berkeley, California, on December 6th, 1956 and is best known as the lead guitarist and co-founder of the band R.E.M. His early years were spent moving between Los Angeles and San Francisco before the family settled in Georgia. His school years were spent in the same region and he eventually studied at Emory University and the University of Georgia before dropping out of education. While working at a record store in Athens, Georgia, Buck met future band mate Michael Stipe and the pair began writing songs together, eventually in conjunction with Mike Mills and Bill Berry.

R.E.M. (as they became) quickly became a major attraction on the local and regional touring circuit, which led to them recording a single (*Radio Free Europe*) and eventually their first EP called *Chronic Town* was released on the IRS label. The group's first full album was *Murmur*, and received considerable acclaim upon its 1983 release, with *Rolling Stone* magazine naming it their album of the year. Following this early success, the band continued to develop through several subsequent albums and by the mid-1980s were signed to Warner Brothers. The album *Document* is regarded as their breakthrough recording with the single *The One I Love* getting into the top 20 both in the US and abroad.

By the early 1990s, R.E.M. were very popular commercially and the single *Losing My Religion* received heavy airplay on many radio stations worldwide. The album containing this single, *Out of Time,* was their seventh recording and sold over 4 million copies in the US alone. The second single, *Shiny Happy People*, was also a great commercial success. The album was not supported by a major tour, however, and the group instead played several one-off shows.

The group continued to record through the 1990s and eventually organised a large-scale tour in 1995 which was highly successful. After a number of health scares within the band personnel they re-signed with Warner Brothers for an increased advance and recorded the 1996 album *New Adventures in Hi-Fi*.

R.E.M. finally disbanded in September 2011 and Peter Buck has since recorded several solo albums. His latest project called *Arthur Buck* is due to produce a recording in 2018

Guitar style, instruments and equipment

Peter Buck's guitar style is quite diverse, although clearly influenced by artists such as John Lennon and Roger McGuinn of The Bryds. Although not a player who takes extended solos, he occasionally uses intricate country guitar influences in his playing.

Peter Buck has used a wide variety of guitars over the years including Fender Telecasters and a Rickenbacker 360 (he has also used Rickenbacker 325s and 330s). He has also regularly recorded with a Gibson Les Paul and a wide variety of acoustic instruments.

For amplification, Buck has favoured the Vox AC30 and a Savage Blitz 50 amp amongst others. His effects arsenal includes units such as the Pro Co Rat distortion, Maxon Analog Delay and a Line 6 DL4 delay alongside a number of Fulltone boost pedals and overdrives

Recommended Listening

R.E.M. – *Automatic for the People*

R.E.M. – *Murmur*

R.E.M. – *Document*

R.E.M. – *Out of Time*

This first idea uses a mixture of strummed open position chords and picked arpeggios which is very typical of Peter Buck's playing with R.E.M. In bar one, an open position Em chord is strummed just fractionally ahead of the first beat and is followed by a short arpeggiated figure in the same chord form. This approach continues in the next few bars. Note the use of the open E string in the second bar to create a Dus2 chord.

A short two-note bass run in bar eight leads into the chorus section in bar nine where an open position G major is used to contrast with the earlier arpeggios. To add a little extra variety there is an 1/8th note figure in bars twelve and sixteen to lead back into the subsequent chord. Make sure to let all the indicated arpeggios ring into each other when required and add a little tremolo effect to your guitar tone.

Example 3a

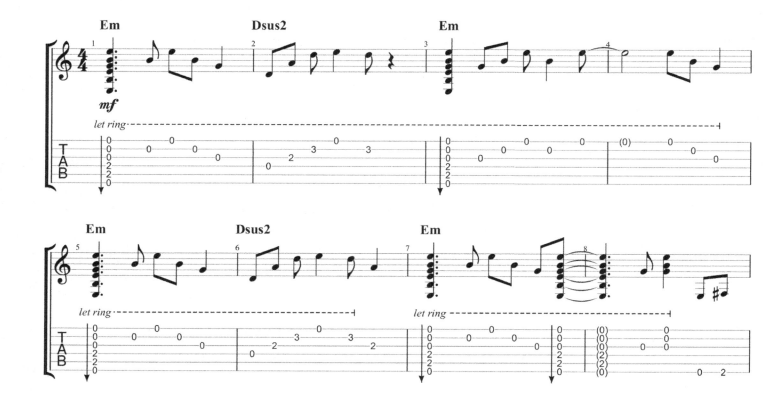

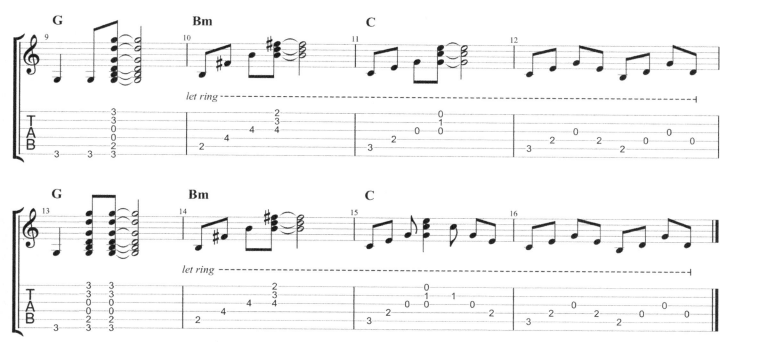

The next example is entirely played in 1/8th notes and uses the open E string as a drone throughout the first eight bars. The use of the open string here is very reminiscent of a number of late 60s US rock bands such as The Byrds. In the second section of the lick that begins in bar five, a similar approach is used in the first two bars with the drone note becoming the D note on the second string at the third fret (D).

In the final two bars, a more conventional arpeggio approach (without a drone string) is adopted using an open position C major chord. Remember to hold down these chord shapes while you are playing the arpeggios to allow some ringing between the individual notes.

Example 3b

Example 3c again features the use of arpeggios, now with higher register inversions than used in the previous examples. This can be an effective way to construct additional guitar parts, especially if there is another guitarist using open position chords at the same time. The lick begins with a 7th position G major triad (a common chord substitution for Em) and then progresses to a Dsus arpeggio in the fifth position in bar two. In bars three and four you play the same G major triad you used in the first bar, but now with a slightly syncopated rhythm involving a tied note over the bar line between the last two bars.

After the repeat, the lick continues with more high register arpeggios based around the 7th position on the fingerboard following the underlying chords of G, Bm and C. As with the earlier section, there is a tied note held over the bar line between the final two bars. These arpeggio patterns don't always have to be played identically on repeated sections, so feel free to embellish or change them slightly as heard in the accompanying audio file.

Example 3c

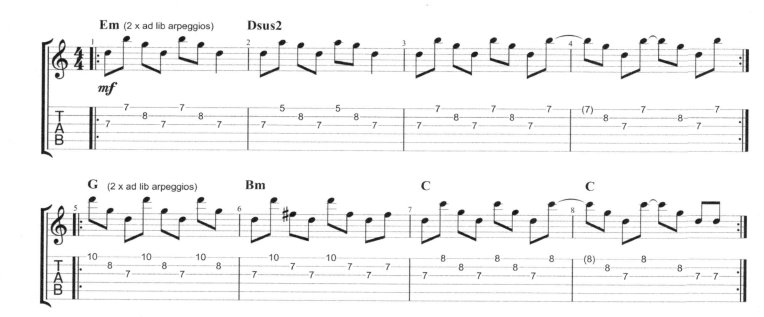

This next example is simple sounding, but still effective in the context of the track. The first four bars use triad forms on the top three strings and really cut through the mix clearly with the bright guitar sound. Rhythmically, just sustain each chord for three beats in each bar.

In the second part of the lick beginning at bar five, the chords are all extended to four notes and again stay on the top strings to keep a bright, clear sounding tone. There is nothing hard to play here, but make sure you keep solid time with the rhythm track.

Example 3d

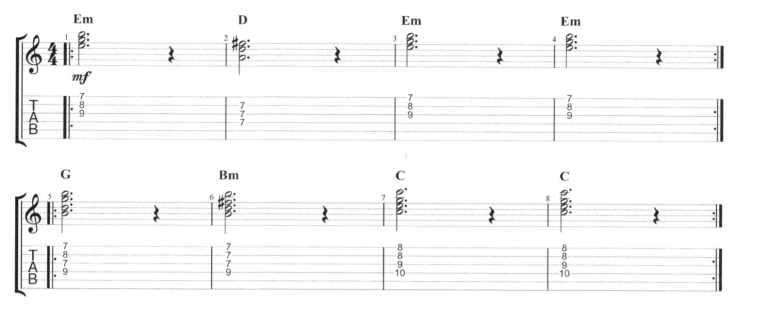

Repeated 1/8th note patterns make very effective rhythm guitar parts and this next example uses them throughout. The lick also revisits the drone string concept seen in Example 3b and the open top E string is used in every bar on each off-beat. Using a slightly overdriven guitar tone will really enhance the sound of the open string too.

As the underlying chords change, you'll see the notes that fall directly onto the beats change to fit the harmony, while the open string drone remains on every other 1/8th note. Remember to play the indicated slides, such as in the first two bars, as this really enhances the sound of the whole lick.

Example 3e

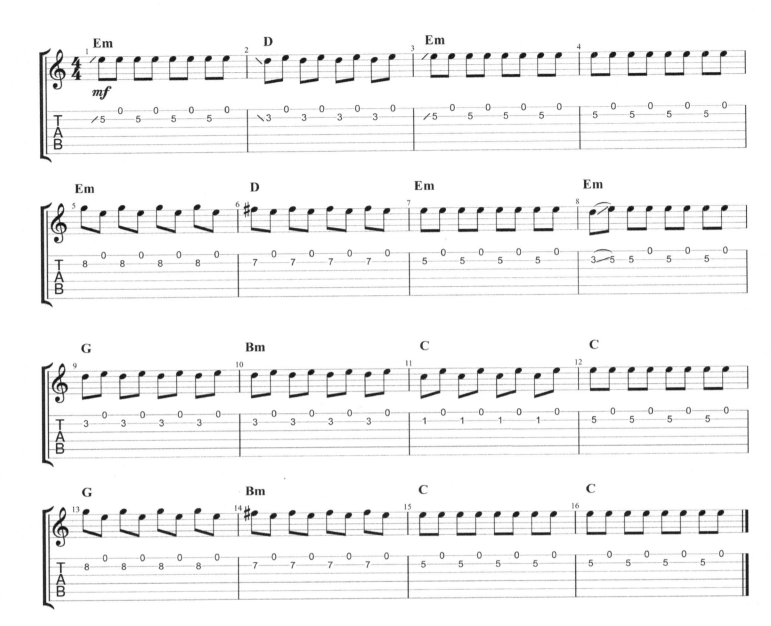

Billy Duffy (The Cult)

Billy Duffy was born William Henry Duffy in Manchester, England, on the 12th May 1961. He grew up in the Manchester area and began playing guitar at the age of fourteen, influenced by the popular hard rock acts of the day. By the late 1970s his interest had moved onto the emerging punk rock music scene and he became interested in groups such as the New York Dolls and The Stooges.

After Duffy left school, he moved to London with a band called the Studio Sweethearts and when they broke up, began collaborating with the singer Ian Astbury, who at the time was fronting The Southern Death Cult. Suitably enamoured with each other's musical skills, the duo quickly formed Death Cult, which was then shortened to simply The Cult.

The Cult's album *Love* produced the hit single *She Sells Sanctuary* and over the next few years Duffy and Astbury developed the band's sound into a very commercially successful rock format with albums like *Sonic Temple* which was released in 1988. He and Astbury had by now also moved to Los Angeles. After recording the album simply entitled *The Cult* in 1992, Astbury left the group and there followed a four-year period of inactivity, during which Duffy worked with a number of other musicians.

The Cult reformed in 1999 and signed a new recording contract with Atlantic Records leading to the next album, *Beyond Good and Evil*. Ultimately, the group once again disbanded and it wasn't until 2006 that they worked together again. The Cult continue to play together as of 2018.

Duffy has also worked with a number of other groups including Circus Diablo and The Kings of Chaos. Outside of his musical activities, Duffy has also contributed to several TV programmes and film projects and was a judge on Bodog Music's Battle of the Bands.

Guitar style, instruments and equipment

Billy Duffy's playing is steeped in traditional rock guitar stylings and he is an especially strong and well-defined rhythm guitarist with a notable skill for coming up with unique sounding guitar parts.

Duffy is most closely associated with the Gretsch White Falcon guitar (perhaps a surprising choice for a rock guitarist), although he uses other more commonplace rock instruments such as a Gibson Les Paul Custom quite regularly.

For amplification, Duffy has favoured Marshall and other similarly toned amplifiers as well as using Vox AC30s and Roland JC-120s for cleaner tones. He uses a multitude of different effects pedals covering flanging, chorus, delay and phasing. The manufacturers of his pedals include, Boss, Jim Dunlop, Klon and Lovepedal. He uses Dunlop Herco picks.

Recommended Listening

The Cult – *Sonic Temple*

The Cult – *Love*

The Cult – *Electric*

The Cult – *Beyond Good and Evil*

Using a constant drone from the open D string, this is a typical-sounding Billy Duffy lick. It is constructed around a mostly descending melody which is played on the G string exclusively. The combination of the two adjacent strings has an almost sitar like sound to it, enhanced with the use of a flanger effect on the guitar tone.

The melody itself is composed from the Mixolydian scale. Make sure to play all the notated slides as they are crucial to the overall sound and effectiveness of the idea. Use an overdriven guitar tone and some delay (preferably set to match the tempo of the song).

Example 4a

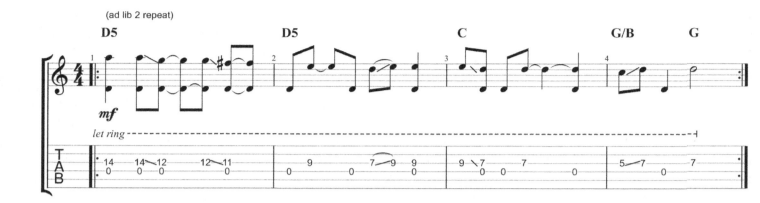

The next example is similar to a classic rock guitar rhythm guitar part. Beginning with steady 1/8th notes played in the classic 'power chord' interval of a perfect fifth (the combined D and A notes) the notes remain consistent even when the underlying chords change from D to C and then G/B to G. Be sure to keep your time steady with the drums when playing this section of the lick. You will need to palm-mute the first eight bars as well.

In bar nine the rhythm changes to long sustained power chords interspersed with 1/8th note, 1/4 note, and some full six string G chords, such as those seen in bars twelve and sixteen. Use an overdriven guitar tone with plenty of sustain and play the lick on the bridge pickup.

Example 4b

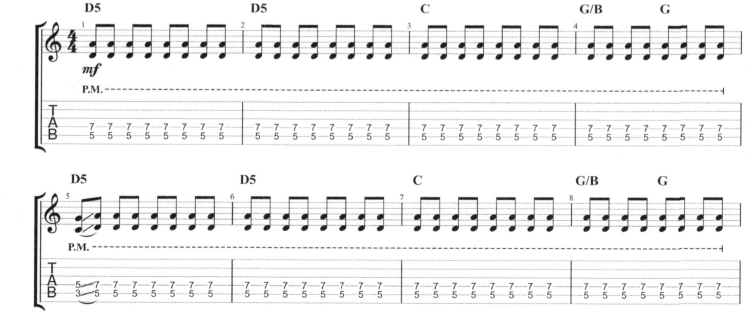

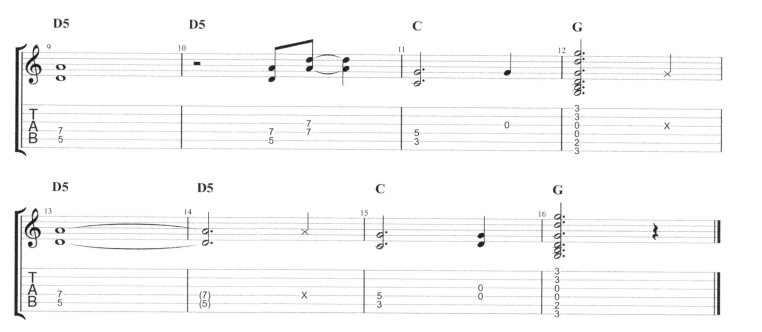

Palm-muting is used once again in this example as well as the repeated 1/8th note pattern seen in the last lick. This example uses some higher register intervals than the previous lick, and watch out for the note changes in bars three and four which reflect the chord changes. The first section from bars one to four is all played on the D, G and B string for a consistent tone.

The second portion of this lick uses a harmonic addition/accent on the third beat of each bar, where you add an extra note to the three-note structures used elsewhere. You may find it easier to play this whole lick with downstrokes rather than use alternate picking.

Example 4c

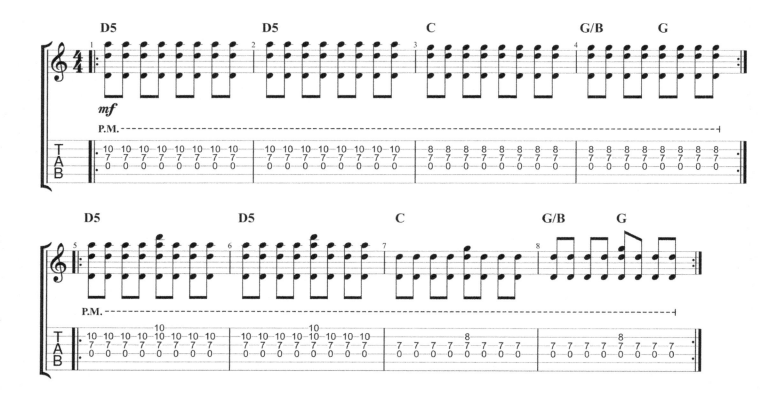

Example 4d again uses three note structures, but now with a more syncopated rhythm. You may need to refer to the audio to get the timing right. The entire lick is played on the D, G and B strings and involves playing a hammer-on on the B string on the first beat in bar one. Try fingering the hammer-on with your first and fourth fingers. The open D string is again used as a form of drone and is similar to Example 4a.

You may find that playing with downstrokes works best when playing this example. Follow the drums closely so as not to rush the tempo.

Example 4d

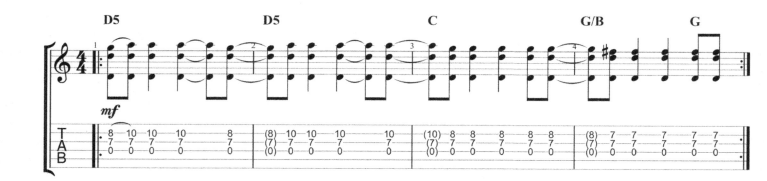

The final Billy Duffy-style idea purposely uses a cleaner guitar tone than the other examples and would work well recorded under more overdriven guitar sounds to thicken up a final mix. There is nothing particularly demanding to play here, as just triads or open positions chords are used. These types of rhythm guitar parts are often crucial to a finished recording and should be played very accurately.

In the first three bars, the chords are sustained for the whole bar and in bars four for just three beats. When playing guitar parts like this, aim to achieve a consistent volume between each chord and avoid either playing too loud or too soft.

Example 4e

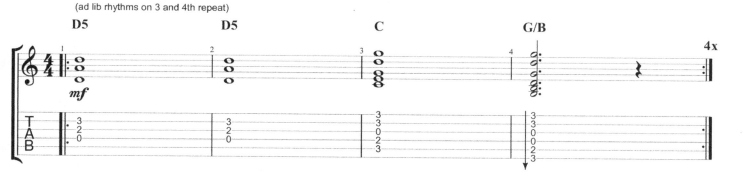

Johnny Marr (The Smiths)

Johnny Marr was born John Martin Maher on the 31st October 1963 in Manchester, England, to Irish immigrant parents. Taking a keen interest in music at an early age, he had formed his first band by the age of 13 and worked with several others before he formed The Smiths with singer Morrisey in 1982.

The Smiths became very successful commercially due in no small part to Marr's highly distinctive guitar work, which although reminiscent of some late 1960s pop bands (e.g. The Bryds) was really in a class of its own. The Smiths recorded four studio albums for the label Rough Trade Records and had several singles enter the top 20 in the UK Singles Charts.

The song writing partnership of Marr and Morrisey won the group a huge fan following and, despite splitting up in 1987 due to internal differences, their music remains highly popular. The group never reformed despite several offers to do so, and Marr has since gone on to work with a variety of other bands and musical projects.

Marr is also a much sought-after session musician working with the likes of The Pretenders, The The, and The Cribs. He has also worked with Talking Heads and even the film composer Hans Zimmer. His playing style has earned him high ranking in a number of musical polls including fourth best guitarist of the last 30 years in a BBC music poll. NME music magazine hailed him as a 'godlike genius' who is always keen to push his musical boundaries.

Guitar style, instruments and equipment

Johnny Marr's playing style is influenced by a variety of guitar players including Neil Young and George Harrison and he frequently uses open tunings and open string voicings to create his signature guitar parts. He favours arpeggio style parts in many of his recordings and enjoys creating chiming chord sequences using open strings wherever possible.

His most commonly played instruments include a Fender Jaguar and a Rickenbacker 330 (he also uses a Rickenbacker 12 string model – the 360). Fender have produced a Johnny Marr Signature version Jaguar in his honour. His other guitars include a Gibson Les Paul and ES-335 model.

Marr's amplification choice is generally a Fender amplifier and he has used Twin Reverbs, Deluxe Reverbs and Bassman during his career. At times he has also recorded with a Roland JC-120 and a Vox AC30 combo.

For effects, Marr uses mostly Boss units, particularly the company's CE-2 chorus pedal and OD-2 overdrive. He also uses a TW-1 wah wah pedal on occasion.

Recommended Listening

The Smiths – *Strangeways, Here We Come*

The Smiths – *Hatful of Hollow*

The Smiths – *Louder Than Bombs*

The Smiths – *The Queen is Dead*

Using a clean guitar tone, this example is arpeggio based and constructed around the upper portions of common open string chords. You may find that examples like this are easier to play if you finger full chord shapes rather than just the notes indicated in the music. Experiment by using a pick or a hybrid of pick and fingers if that feels more comfortable. Use a bright guitar tone and the bridge pickup for a little extra bite in the guitar tone.

Example 5a

The next is another example of how a simple sounding guitar part can really enhance a track. Beginning with an open position E major chord in bar one (with an added 9th on the top E string) it is played with a syncopated rhythm. Use a semi-overdriven sound to recreate the tone heard in the recording.

In bar four, note the use of a doubled G note on both the open third (G) string and the fifth fret on the D string. Try to let each chord ring for as long as possible too.

Example 5b

Johnny Marr has often recorded with a tremolo effect added to his guitar sound. Set the timing of the tremolo sweep to match the tempo of the song to achieve the sound in the recording.

Example 5c

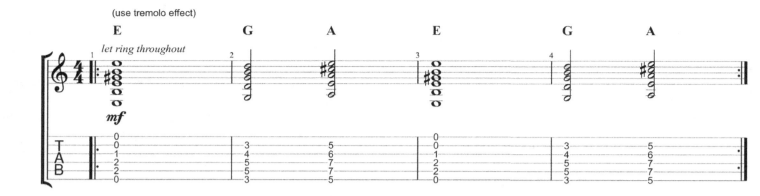

Example 5d uses a simple motif which involves sliding between diatonic intervals mostly on the second (B) string. In bar one, the E note (on the open top string) is doubled on the fifth fret of the second string, then slid down to the third fret to accommodate the G major chord. Use your first finger for these slides so that you keep in position for each new chord in the progression.

Rhythmically, the whole lick is a combination of alternating 1/4 and 1/ 8th notes. Refer to the audio example to get the exact timing if you need to.

Example 5d

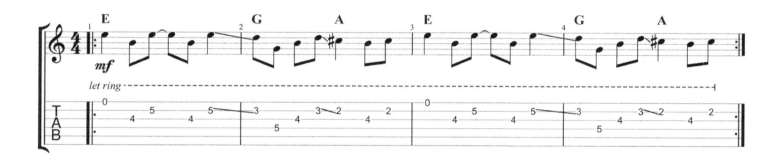

1/8th note chord accents are used in this lick to punctuate the chord progression. This is a simple, yet very effective guitar part and would work well with other more syncopated rhythm guitar tracks.

Keep the chord rhythms precise and listen to the drums to help you keep a steady tempo throughout. Use a fairly bright guitar tone and back off the overdrive to achieve the right sound.

Example 5e

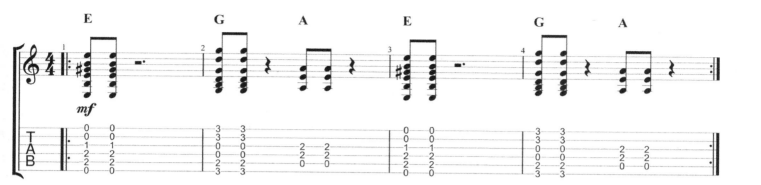

John Squire (The Stone Roses)

Jonathan Thomas Squire was born on the 24th November 1962 in Altrincham, England. He developed a keen interest in art at an early age and met eventual Stone Roses singer Ian Brown at school. Squire was largely self-taught on the guitar and only took a small number of guitar lessons, preferring to find his own voice on the instrument. He found a shared interest for punk rock music in Ian Brown, listening to bands like The Clash and The Sex Pistols, and this led them to eventually form their own band, The Patrol.

Squire and Brown co-founded The Stone Roses in 1983 and became a highly influential group after their debut album *The Stone Roses* in 1989. That year proved to be very successful for the band with headlining concerts and critical acclaim for their album. The group also won four NME awards including Single of the Year for their song *Fools Gold*.

By the 1990s, The Stone Roses were well established and seen as the founding fathers of the fast-developing Britpop scene (they were a formative influence on bands like Oasis). The group released their second album, *Second Coming* in 1992 to a mixed reaction from critics and fans alike. The album was heavier than their first recording and based more around blues-rock. Its reception, combined with internal feuds, led Squire to leave the group in 1996.

Squire formed The Seahorses and released one album before disbanding completely and recording two solo albums. In the following years Squire devoted his time to the art world and it was not until he settled his personal differences with Ian Brown that they reunited in 2012 and undertook an extensive reunion tour. Squire is primarily now a professional artist with several highly successful exhibitions to his name, both in the UK and abroad.

Guitar style, instruments and equipment

John Squire's guitar style contains strong elements of funk guitar, using muted strings and triadic chord forms frequently. He also uses double stops, arpeggios and harmonies played in diatonic intervals in many songs.

He has used a Gretsch Country Gentleman 'Chet Atkins' model and the more typical Gibson Les Pauls and Fender solid bodies (Telecasters and Jaguars etc). Fender also produced a signature John Squire Jaguar model, although he has also played a Hofner T45 guitar.

His choice of amplifiers has ranged from a Fender Twin Reverb through to Mesa Boogies and a Vox AC30 amplifier. For effects, he favours pedals made by Ibanez and Boss, covering overdrive, delay, chorusing and modulation effects like phasing and flanging. Squire also uses a wah wah pedal on occasion.

Recommended Listening

The Stone Roses – *The Stone Roses*

The Stone Roses – *Second Coming*

The Stone Roses – *The Complete Stone Roses*

The Seahorses – *Do It Yourself*

This first John Squire lick uses three-string arpeggios to outline the chords, beginning with an E minor triad in the 7th position in bar one. In bar two, the top note descends by one fret to outline an Em6 chord.

Let each arpeggio ring out for as long as possible and use the bridge pickup with a bright guitar tone. The lick concludes with a strummed Em chord.

Example 6a

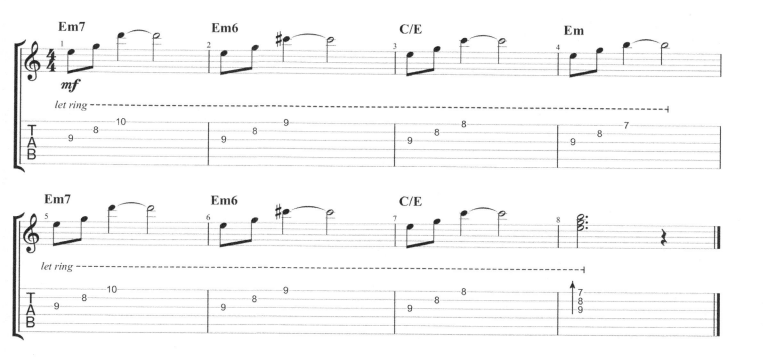

In the next sequence, beginning with Em7 in bar one, the two lower notes of the structure remain the same before the top note descends by a semitone in bar two to create the Em6.

The descending top note melody is an effective way to outline the song's chord progression and is a John Squire signature move. Note that each chord is strummed for the duration of three beats in each bar.

Example 6b

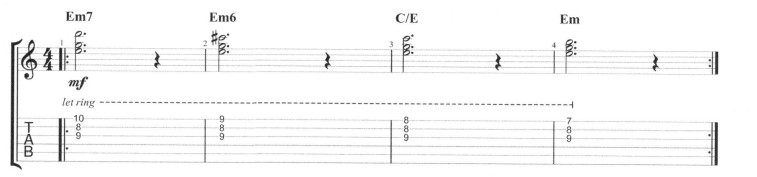

Using a heavy tremolo effect, the next riff uses a similar approach to the previous one, but with lower register chord voicings and adding open strings for extra resonance. Once again, each chord is sustained for three beats in every bar.

As with the previous example, the top note of the first three chords descends by one fret at a time to clearly outline the chord progression.

Example 6c

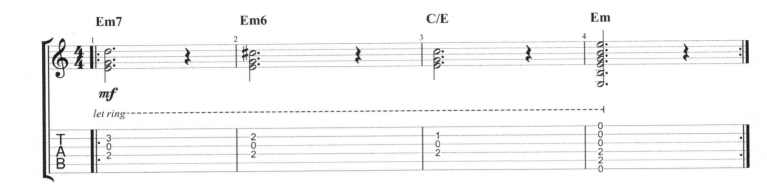

Sounding a little like the James Bond theme, Example 6d uses single notes rather than chords that are carefully chosen to follow the harmony of the song. Beginning with a D note on the fifth string, the line descends to the note B. Use a little palm muting to achieve the sound heard in the audio and add some overdrive to your guitar tone to make sure the notes have plenty of attack.

The rhythm remains consistent throughout with a dotted 1/4 note and 1/8th note rhythm followed by a regular 1/4 note. A simple but very effective guitar part.

Example 6d

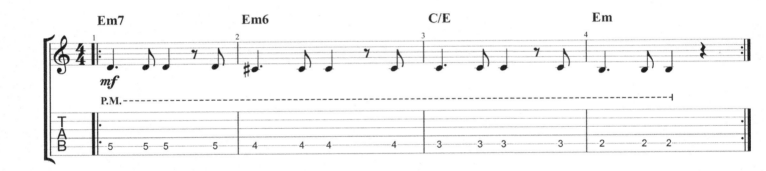

This next arpeggio-based idea once again outlines the song's harmony and is played entirely on the top three strings to create a bright ringing sound. Everything is played in steady 1/8th notes, so ensure that you keep the arpeggios even sounding and in tempo.

Let each arpeggio ring for as long as possible and add a little reverb to achieve the recorded sound.

Example 6e

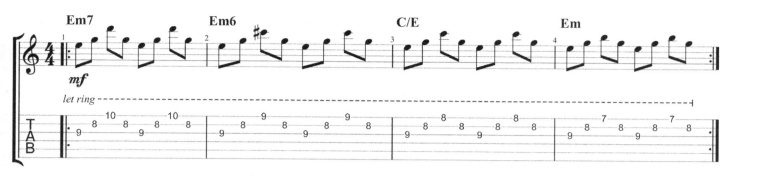

Jonny Greenwood (Radiohead)

Jonathan Richard Guy Greenwood was born on 5th November 1971 in Oxford, England. His first exposure to music was Classical and Baroque, and he played recorder and studied viola, keyboards and harmonica before turning to guitar.

While attending school in Oxford he met singer Thom Yorke and guitarist Ed O'Brian and joined their band "On A Friday" in which he initially played keyboards (and harmonica) before switching to lead guitar. Greenwood also studied music at A level and went on to enrol on a degree in music and psychology at Oxford University. During this time, On A Friday were signed to EMI, changed their name to Radiohead, and Greenwood dropped out of his university course.

Radiohead quickly attained commercial and artistic success with their first single *Creep* in 1992 and their debut album *Pablo Honey* was released in 1993. The follow up album *The Bends* cemented their initial acclaim and, by the time of the release of their third album, *OK Computer*, Radiohead were an international act with a major following. The groups' final album for EMI *Hail to the Thief* was released in 2003 and was a mixed electronic and rock recording. Since then, they have released their music via torrent and pay-to-download websites, rather than utilise a traditional record company.

Greenwood's contribution to Radiohead's music has been massive and has included orchestrated string arrangements, along with loops and samples in their music. The most recent Radiohead album was 2016's *A Moon Shaped Pool* which features Greenwoods orchestrations prominently throughout.

Radiohead have sold more than 30 million albums and were nominated to the Rock & Roll Hall of Fame in 2017 and 2018. Greenwood has composed and recorded film scores, and collaborated with artists such as Andy Mackay, Bernard Butler and Bryan Ferry.

Guitar style, instruments and equipment

As a skilled multi-instrumentalist, Greenwood brings many influences to his playing, with rock, classical, jazz, hip-hop and reggae elements evident in his music.

His main instrument is a Fender Telecaster Plus with Lace Sensor pickups, although he also uses a Fender Starcaster and Gibson Les Paul. Greenwood has used a wide variety of amplifiers including a Vox AC30, and various Fender combos including a Super Reverb and a '65 Twin Reverb. He uses a variety of effects including an Akai E1 Headrush delay, a Dementer Tremulator Tremolo unit and a DOD Envelope filter.

Recommended Listening

Radiohead – *Kid A*

Radiohead – *In Rainbows*

Radiohead – *OK Computer*

Radiohead – *The Bends*

Our first Johnny Greenwood idea is constructed from 1/8th note arpeggios based on the chord progression and uses a clean guitar tone throughout. There shouldn't be any problems here technically, although be careful with your picking to ensure all notes have an equal volume. Try playing this on your neck pickup for a warmer tone.

Example 7a

A tremolo pedal is added in Example 7b and each strum is played just fractionally ahead of the beat to ensure that the chords all stay in time. In bar five, the D major chord is played as a Dsus2 using the open top E string. This is a common substitute for a regular D major chord in Indie rock.

After the A major in bar seven, the single-note arpeggio idea in the final bar uses a 1/4 note triplet rhythm. Listen to the audio recording to help get the timing if you need to.

Example 7b

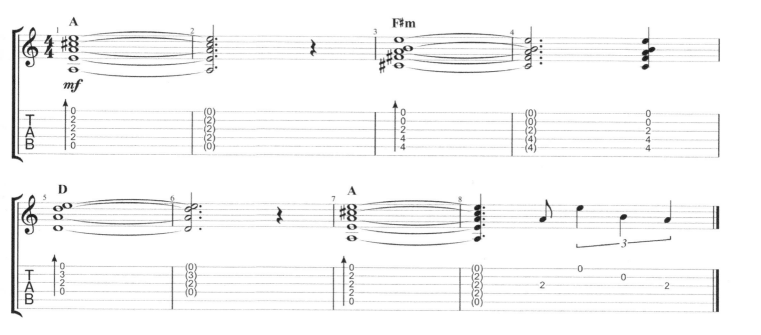

Triads are used in the first three bars of this next riff before the five-note voicing for F#m in bar four. In bars five to eight, the rhythms become a little more involved and add variety to the guitar part. Although all the chords are commonplace, it shows how they can be used to create an effective guitar part in a slower tempo song.

Use a warmer guitar sound that's just on the edge of breaking up, and experiment with some compression to let the notes of each chord ring a bit longer.

Example 7c

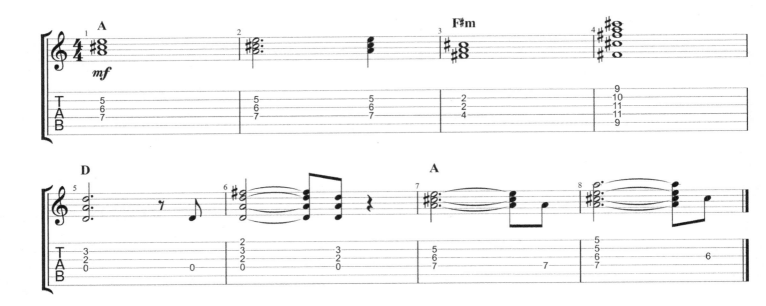

A delay is used in the next example to create a doubling effect not unlike that used by The Edge from U2. If your delay pedal allows you to set dotted 1/8th notes, then you should be able to recreate the sound easily. The lick is played in steady 1/8th notes, but the dotted delay effect creates a much more sophisticated part.

Use your bridge pickup for this lick and add a little reverb to create a more atmospheric tone.

Example 7d

This final Johnny Greenwood idea is a simple, driving 1/8th note part on the root note of each chord. Although guitar parts like this sound simple, they enhance a track considerably by giving a thicker texture to the harmony.

Example 7e

Joey Santiago (Pixies)

Joey Santiago was born Joseph Alberto Santiago in Manila, Philippines, on June 10th 1965, and emigrated from the Philippines with his family in 1972. The family eventually settled in Massachusetts where Santiago attended high school and later Wilbraham & Monson Academy. His first instrument was the Hammond organ, but at the age of 9 he shifted to guitar and became influenced by artists such as The Velvet Underground and Iggy Pop.

After enrolling at the University of Massachusetts to study economics, Santiago met future Pixies front man Charles Thompson and struck up a friendship based on their musical interests. After a brief student exchange trip to Puerto Rico, Santiago and Thompson both left college and moved to Boston, where in 1986 they formed the Pixies.

The Pixies signed to the English label 4AD in 1987 and released their first album *Come on Pilgrim*. They began touring heavily and, after recording a further two albums – *Surfer Rosa* and *Doolittle* – tensions within the band caused Santiago to leave in 1989. After a short break the band re-united and recorded a further two albums, *Bossanova* and *Trompe le Monde*.

The Pixies broke up once more in 1992 due to continued personal tensions. Following this, Santiago worked and collaborated with many other musicians and became involved in film scoring and TV work.

In 2004 after some initial communication between the various band members, the Pixies reunited and in 2016 released their sixth studio album called *Head Carrier*. Santiago also continues to work in TV and film production.

Guitar style, instruments and equipment

Joey Santiago's guitar style is an amalgam of many different musical influences, including classic rock, country and jazz guitar to name a few. He is also a keen experimenter with guitar effects and feedback techniques.

Santiago primarily uses Gibson guitars, including a Les Paul Goldtop, an ES-345 and a Gibson Black Beauty. He has also used PRS and Duesenberg guitars.

For amplification he favours either Marshall or Fender tube amplifiers such as the Fender Vibrolux and the Marshall JCM800 model. For effects, he uses a wide variety of modulation and delay effects made by manufactures such as Boss, Empress, TC Electronic and Fulltone.

Recommended Listening

Pixies – *Doolittle*

Pixies – *Surfer Rosa*

Pixies – *Bossanova*

Pixies – *Trompe le Monde*

This first Joey Santiago riff uses barre chord shapes that create an effective rhythm guitar part. Each chord is held for the duration of three beats which helps to contrast with the 1/8th note feel of the bass part.

A "less is more" approach to rhythm guitar is often the most effective way of getting a part to sit well in a track and this example is a case in point. Use a clean guitar tone throughout.

Example 8a

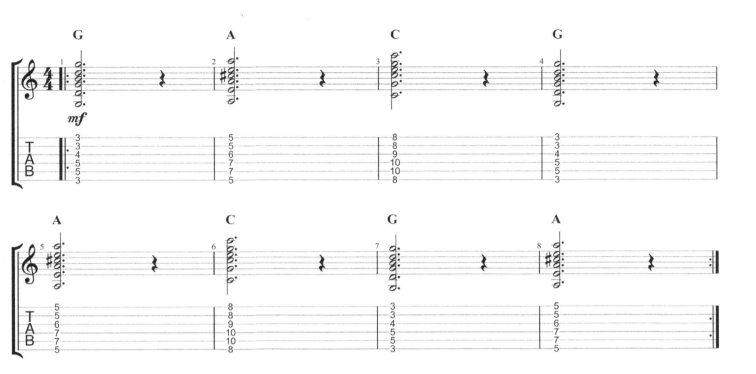

Here's another 1/8th note idea that creates a great driving feel and mirrors the bass part by playing root notes. Use a slightly overdriven, but not an excessively distorted tone.

Example 8b

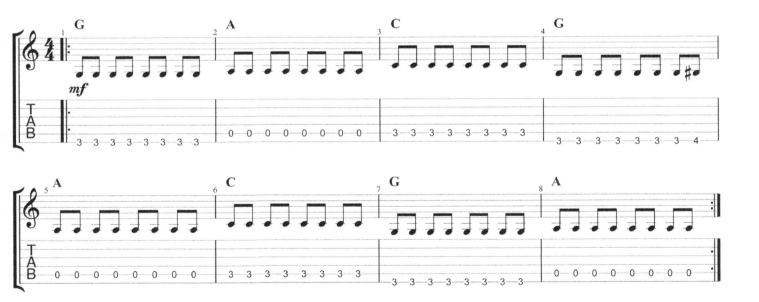

Taking the previous example a stage further, the next Santiago-style phrase again uses an 1/8th note pattern throughout, but this time with more melodic variation. In bars one and two, use your first finger to bar across the top two strings and use downstrokes exclusively.

On the C chord in bars three and six, finger the double-stop with your first and third fingers and make sure you mute any un-played strings with the heel of your picking hand.

Example 8c

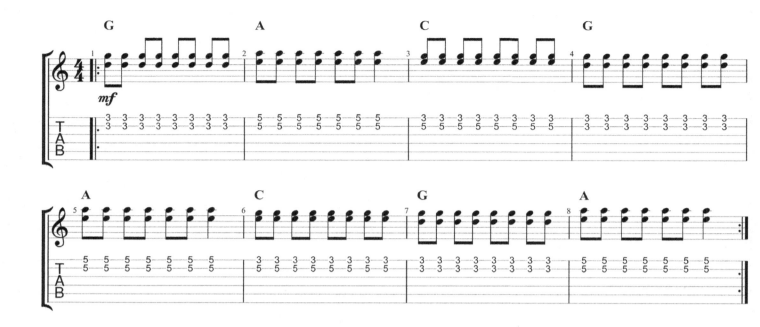

Example 8d uses the open G string as a drone note on each chord and the entire phrase is played on just the two middle strings. Ensure that the open G string is played on every other 1/8th note throughout.

In guitar parts like this, it is important that the volume of both the fretted and open strings are kept the same, so make sure you play everything evenly.

Example 8d

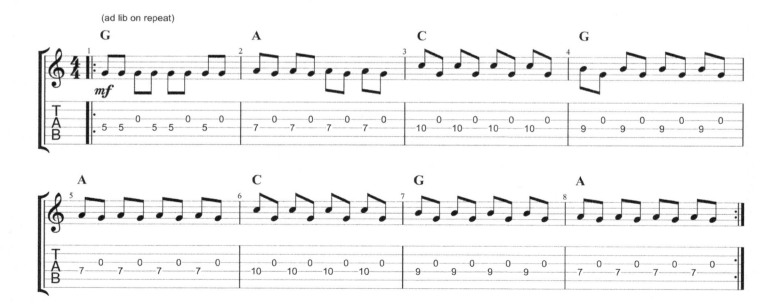

The final Joey Santiago riff has a funky off-beat feel and works well against the steady 1/8th note feel of the backing track. Watch that you mute the notated "x" notes as this adds considerably to the effectiveness of the lick.

All the chords are played as triads on the top three strings and you will need to mute the un-played strings to avoid any extraneous noise. On the repeat, try to vary and embellish the written rhythm for a little variety. Refer to the audio for some ideas.

Example 8e

Kevin Shields (My Bloody Valentine)

Kevin Patrick Shields was born in New York City on the 21st May, 1963. His family were of Irish descent and had emigrated from Ireland in the 1950s. While he was still young, the family moved back to Ireland in 1973 and settled in Dublin where Shields received his first guitar as a Christmas present from his parents in 1979.

Shields began playing with local bands in the Dublin area and after developing a friendship with drummer Colm Ó Cíosóig they joined a punk group called The Complex. After the sudden departure of the lead singer from The Complex they formed A Life in the Day. This lasted until 1981 when Shields and Ó Cíosóig formed My Bloody Valentine (MBV), the group that Shields is best known for.

MBV signed to Creation Records in 1988 and released several EPs along with two studio albums, *Isn't Anything* and *Loveless*. Loveless is widely regarded as their best album and one of the most significant alternative rock recordings of the 1990s. Due to increasing production costs, Creation dropped MBV from its label and in 1992 they signed to Island Records, although much of their recorded work was not released by the new label.

After two members of the band left in 1995, Shields found himself unable to continue and largely withdrew from group activities. He did, however, collaborate with other musicians and work as a session musician with other artists until MBV reformed in 2008. A new album, *m b v*, was released on their website in February 2013 and a world tour followed shortly after. Shields continues to work with MBV and a new album is scheduled for release in 2019.

Guitar style, instruments and equipment

Kevin Shield's guitar style is one of the most recognisable aspects of MBV and he has a textural approach to guitar sounds and playing techniques. He is a fan of effects pedals and uses his tremolo arm extensively to achieve radical pitch bends with chords.

His main guitars are Fender Jaguars and Jazzmasters which he has altered to allow for more manipulation of the tremolo arm. He has also used Yamaha and Ibanez guitars alongside his trademark Fender instruments.

Like many Indie Rock players, Shields favours tube amps like the Vox AC30 and Marshall JCM800 models and on occasion also uses Fender combos and heads.

Shields has many effects at his disposal and his pedalboard is well stocked with various graphic EQs, volume pedals and an array of modulation and delay effects from manufactures such as Boss, Lovetone, ZVex, Electro-Harmonix and Roger Mayer.

Recommended Listening

My Bloody Valentine – *Loveless*

My Bloody Valentine – *m b v*

My Bloody Valentine – *Isn't Anything*

My Bloody Valentine – *EPs 1988-1991*

The tremolo arm gets quite a workout on this first riff and despite it sounding quite simple, you'll need to ensure you use it accurately. In bar one, play the G major chord just before the downbeat with your tremolo arm slightly depressed and then rapidly bring the arm back up to pitch.

In bars two, three and four use the tremolo arm to add some vibrato to each chord. It may take a little practice to get the exact sound, but the resulting effect can really enhance an otherwise straightforward set of chords.

Example 9a

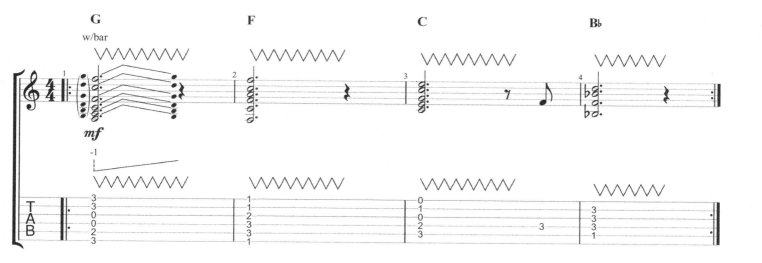

The next riff begins with four sustained chords played with heavy distortion, each lasting for three beats apart from the final one. Try lowering the treble on your guitar a bit to create a darker sound.

The final four bars use the popular rock guitar technique of unison bends between two adjacent strings. Don't worry about pitching the bends perfectly accurately, as the technique sometimes sounds more effective when pitched slightly flat. Use down strokes for this part of the line and begin releasing the bend beginning on the third beat of bar seven.

Example 9b

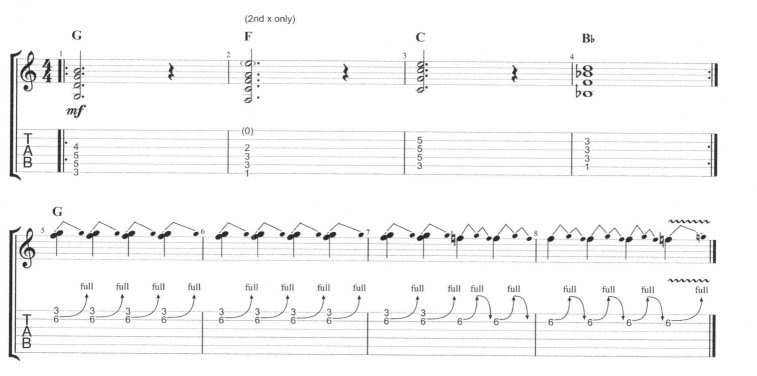

The following arpeggios use the D, G and B strings exclusively. Use a heavily overdriven guitar tone and your bridge pickup for some extra bite. Only the notes on the D string descend as you move through the chord changes.

As always, avoid rushing the time and concentrate on playing accurately against the drums in particular.

Example 9c

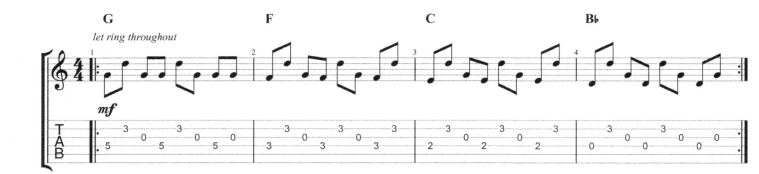

Example 9d returns to the tremolo arm to add vibrato to the indicated chord shapes. All the chords are played as triads and pay attention to the slide leading from bar one into bar two. Use your first finger for this slide and you'll be comfortably in position for the F major chord.

Use an overdriven tone with just enough drive to add some grit, but avoid overly distorting the chord.

Example 9d

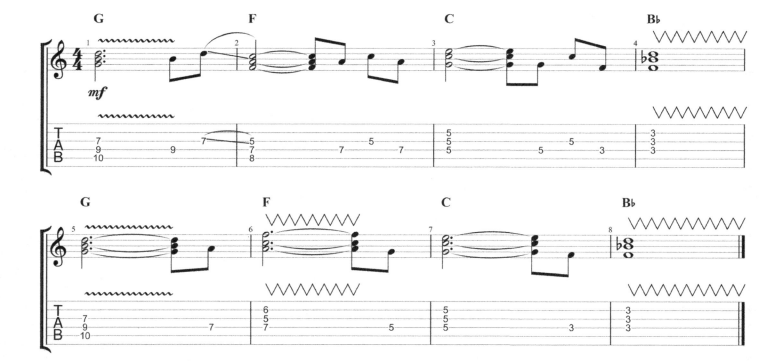

The final Kevin Shields lick contains a repeated octave motif which helps add rhythmic interest to the track. Each octave shape should be played with your first, and either your third or fourth fingers. Be sure to add in the accented ghost notes as they are crucial to the sound of the music.

Octave parts like this are common in many styles of music, but work especially well here as they contrast with the underlying 1/8th note pulse of the track. Mute any unwanted strings and use your neck pickup to create some tonal contrast.

Example 9e

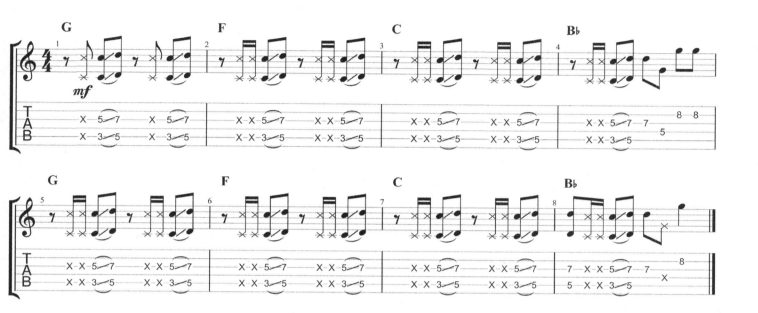

Graham Coxon (Blur)

Graham Leslie Coxon was born on the 12th March, 1969, in Rinteln, Germany. At that time, his father was stationed there, working as a military band leader with the British Army. His family eventually settled back in the UK near Derby, before moving to Colchester, Essex. He went to school at Stanway Comprehensive in Essex and met future Blur bandmate Damon Albarn while a pupil there.

Coxon studied Fine Arts at Goldsmiths College in London for a couple of years while pursuing his growing interest in music and he eventually left the college after his then band (Seymour) became popular. Seymour attracted the attention of Food Records and they signed with the label in March 1990, changing their name to Blur.

Comprising Coxon, Damon Albarn, Alex James and Dave Rowntree, Blur were amongst several groups who followed in the wake of The Stone Roses and brought a new dimension to British guitar-based pop (Britpop) The groups debut album *Leisure* produced two successful singles and gained the group much attention. However, problems with band's US label SBK nearly caused their second album (*Modern Life is Rubbish*) to be re-recorded.

Blur's breakthrough album was *Parklife* in 1994, which propelled the group into stardom with several successful hit singles and much critical acclaim. The group continued their success with several more albums including *The Great Escape*, *Blur* and *Think Tank* (which was recorded minus Coxon). The group's final album, *The Magic Whip*, released on Parlophone in 2015.

Outside of his work with Blur, Coxon has recorded eight solo albums and written scores for TV. He has also produced and re-mixed recordings for several well-known artists in the music industry.

Guitar style, instruments and equipment

Coxon's guitar style is a mixture of diverse influences from blues, classic rock, funk and effects-laden soundscapes. He is as influenced by jazz and RnB as he is by groups like Sonic Youth and post-punk icons Wire.

His main instrument is a Fender Telecaster, but he also plays Gibson guitars including SGs, ES-335s and Les Pauls. Like many guitarists of his generation, he also favours Fender Jaguars and Jazzmasters.

His amplifier of choice is usually a Marshall and, as a self-confessed "pedal junkie", he uses numerous effects to create his signature distortion tones with units made by ProCo and Watsson. These distortion and overdrive pedals are often used together to create a highly individual guitar tone.

Recommended Listening

Blur – *Parklife*

Blur – *13*

Blur – *Modern Life Is Rubbish*

Blur – *Blur*

This first Graham Coxon style riff is busy, but once you have the chord forms under your fingers it should be quite easy to play. It is constructed in two-bar phrases with the rhythm alternating between 1/8th and 1/4 notes.

You could play this with either your neck or bridge pickup, but may find that the neck pickup creates a more rounded guitar tone. Some light overdrive will help get the sound heard on the audio track.

Example 10a

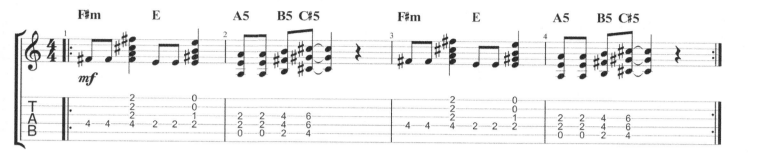

This riff only uses single notes but provides a strong foundation for the chordal harmony. Use an overdriven tone and your bridge pickup and add a little treble if needed. All the notes are just the roots of the indicated chords and the entire lick can be played in the open position of the neck.

As with some earlier ideas, this guitar part mirrors the bassline, so listen carefully and lock into the rhythm.

Example 10b

Here's an example of how you can play the same notes throughout a chord sequence to great effect. This entire riff is played in 1/8th notes by barring across the top two strings at the second fret. Even through the underlying chords change at least twice in each bar, the two notes work well through all of them.

Despite the simplicity of the guitar part, the hardest thing to achieve here is a consistent tone and rhythm.

Example 10c

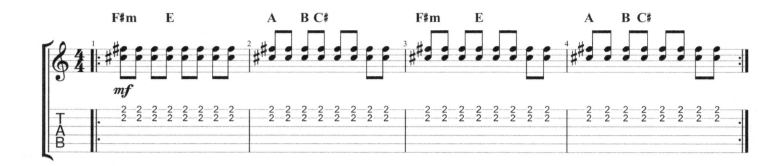

Playing the backbeat of a 4/4 rhythm (accenting the second and fourth beats) is a popular technique and works well in Indie rock. Note that you only play in alternate bars and that the chords are marked staccato (short) to emphasise their percussive nature.

Using a bright tone with added treble will help a rhythm part like this stand out in a recording mix.

Example 10d

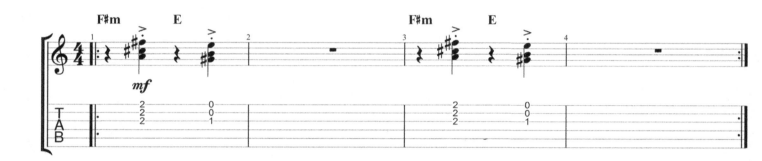

The final example features a rising melody line that is played predominantly in 1/8th notes. The lick only uses the D string (for consistency of tone) and begins on the fourth fret, rising eventually to the 9th. Add a little finger vibrato on the longer notes at the 9th fret.

Example 10e

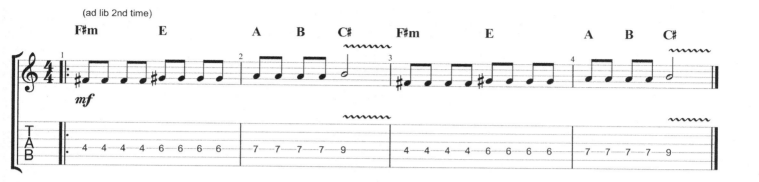

Noel Gallagher (Oasis)

Noel Thomas David Gallagher was born on the 29th May, 1967, in Manchester, England. Gallagher was one of three sons of Irish parents and he began playing guitar at the age of thirteen. After a rather turbulent and difficult childhood and a series of short-term jobs in the construction industry, he began working with the road crew for the band Inspiral Carpets in 1988. While on tour, he heard that his younger brother Liam had formed a group (called The Rain) and when he returned home, he was invited to join them as a songwriter and guitarist.

The Rain changed their name to Oasis and in 1994 released their debut album *Definitely Maybe*. The group quickly gained enormous popularity and were as well known for their music as their off-stage behaviour and partying. The group's second album *(What's the Story) Morning Glory?* reached the top of the charts in several countries and they became one of the leading voices of the Britpop movement.

Their third album *Be Here Now* (1997) was reputedly the fastest selling album in UK history and this period saw the band at their commercial height. However, Britpop was on the decline and, despite the two final Oasis albums (*Don't Believe the Truth* and *Dig Out Your Soul*) being generally well received, Gallagher left the band to pursue a solo career.

His unstable relationship with his brother was beyond repair and Gallagher formed High Flying Birds. This group has released three albums to date and toured the US and Europe in early 2018. At the time of writing an Oasis reunion seems unlikely.

Guitar style, instruments and equipment

Gallagher's playing style owes a great deal to classic British pop and rock guitarists such as Pete Townsend and George Harrison. He is an accomplished rhythm guitarist and is also a confident blues rock style soloist when called upon to improvise.

Gallagher has used a wide variety of guitars including an Epiphone Les Paul, Gibson Les Paul, Fender Telecaster and Epiphone Casino. In recent years he has used a Gibson ES-335 as his main stage guitar.

For amplification he used Marshall 100-watt heads with Oasis at first, before gravitating to smaller combos such as Fender Bandmasters and Princetons. He has also used a combo made by Clark Amplification. Gallagher didn't originally use effects pedals with Oasis, but has since begun using a large number on a pedal board, most particularly the Ibanez Tube Screamer overdrive.

Recommended Listening

Oasis – *Be Here Now*

Oasis – *Definitely Maybe*

Oasis – *Dig Out Your Soul*

Oasis – *(What's the Story) Morning Glory?*

The first guitar part is typical of Noel Gallagher's approach to his rhythm guitar work with Oasis and uses conventional open string chords with either a 7th or 9th degree added. Try to let each chord ring for as long as possible and use an overdriven (although not distorted) tone on your bridge pickup.

Watch out for the anticipated chord "pushes" in bars one and four.

Example 11a

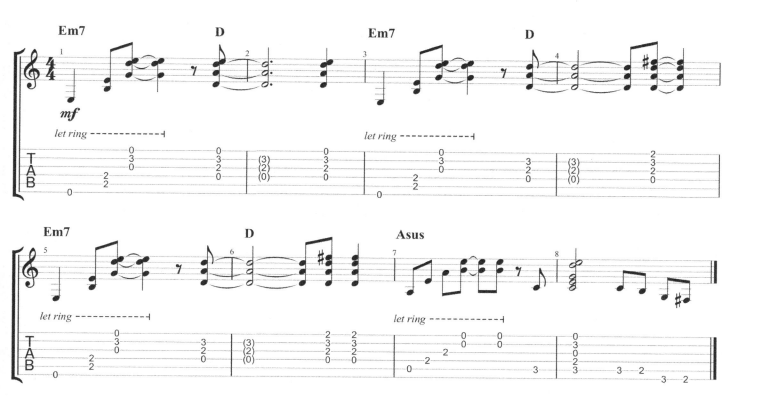

Similar in construction to the previous example, this next rhythm idea emphasises more arpeggio-based figures, primarily played in 1/8th notes. Guitar parts like this are often played in conjunction with examples like the previous one and panned left and right respectively to create a wider stereo sound.

Again, the chords used here contain added 9ths and 7ths to enrich the otherwise basic harmony.

Example 11b

The use of the open E string here (as a drone) is effective in creating tension against the underlying chords. Play all the indicated finger slides on the first beast of each bar and, where possible, use the same finger to ensure a smooth position change. Try playing the part using downstrokes on the B string and upstrokes on the top E string to achieve a consistent dynamic.

You'll find that an overdriven guitar tone really enhances the sound of the open string against the changing notes on the B string.

Example 11c

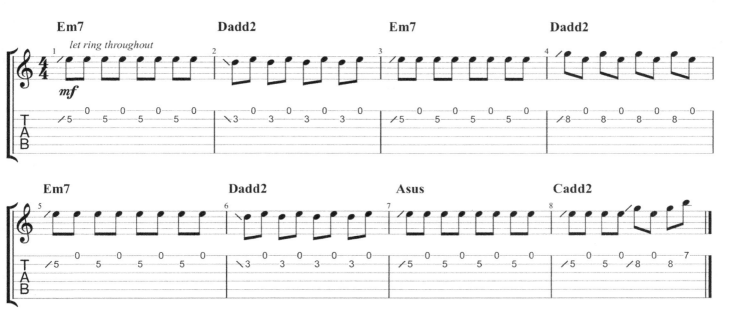

Noel Gallagher tends to play short instrumental breaks instead of extended solos and often uses typical rock pentatonic scale ideas. This next example begins with the use of a repeated (bent) double stop in bars one and two played in the 12th position of the fingerboard. Try using both your third and fourth fingers for the bend here.

Bars three and four use a rhythmic repetition of the E note located at the 14th fret to contrast with the earlier double stops. Add some vibrato in the fourth and eighth bars to enhance the notes.

Example 11d

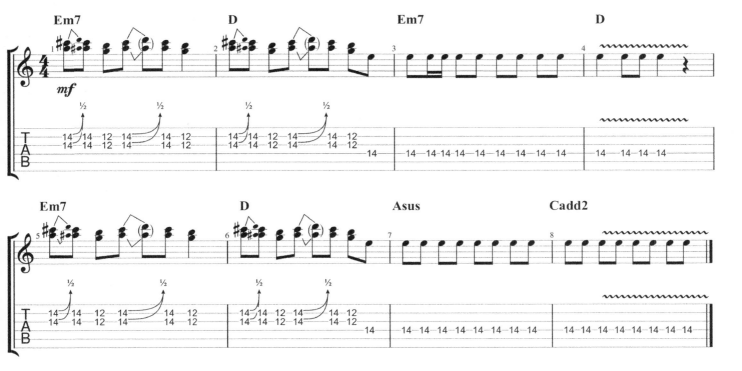

The final idea could easily have come from a Hendrix solo and mostly uses unison string bends in the 12th position. With your first finger on the 12th fret, use your third finger to play the bend on the adjacent G string. It's not necessary to get these bends 100% accurate as they are often used as a special effect, but make sure you get them close to the pitch played on the B string to achieve the best results.

Listen to the recording carefully to hear the subtle changes in rhythm. The first four bars are mostly in 1/4 notes, but the final bar moves to 1/8th notes to peak the solo.

Example 11e

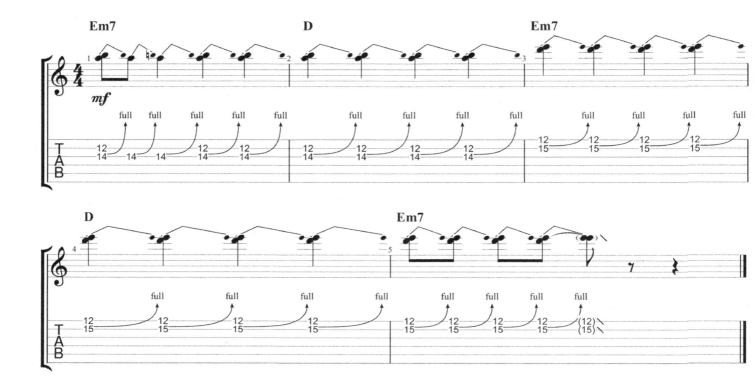

Dave Grohl (Foo Fighters)

David Eric Grohl was born in Warren, Ohio, on 14th January, 1969. His parents divorced when he was 7 and he was raised by his mother in Virginia. He first became interested in the guitar at around 12 years old and is mostly self-taught. He got increasingly into punk music in his teens and by the time he was attending high school he was playing in several different bands.

Around this time, Grohl switched instruments to concentrate on drums and influenced by Led Zeppelin drummer John Bonham's playing, began to get work behind the kit. After auditioning for the Washington based band Scream, Grohl worked with the group until it disbanded in the middle of a tour. Grohl then successfully auditioned for the grunge group Nirvana and became a full-time member. With the success of the album *Nevermind* in 1991, they were propelled to worldwide fame and Grohl became increasingly involved in the songwriting alongside front man Kurt Cobain.

After Cobain's tragic death in 1994, Grohl briefly left the music scene to regroup, but by the end of the year he was recording again and also played drums briefly with Tom Petty. A solo career seemed the next logical step forward for Grohl, but he decided to put together a new band and they subsequently signed with Capitol Records as the Foo Fighters.

Foo Fighters have had incredible international success and won multiple music awards, including four Grammys. They have recorded nine studio albums and sold over 12 million copies in the US alone. They remain a popular concert attraction with their unique blend of alternative rock and post-grunge songwriting.

Guitar style, instruments and equipment

Dave Grohl's guitar style is influenced by a wide variety of musicians, but it has a rock and punk core which is often heard in his rhythm work. He is a talented multi-instrumentalist and his skills on the drum kit undoubtedly influence his playing.

Grohl has been a long-time user of Gibson guitars, in particular the unusual-looking Trini Lopez model. He has also used Gibson SGs and Explorer models. Gibson issued a custom Dave Grohl DG-335 guitar modelled on his old Trini Lopez stage guitar, and he has also used instruments made by Dean, Fender and Gretsch.

Generally favouring tube amplifiers, Grohl has used Vox, Marshall and Mesa Boogie amplifiers alongside boutique makes like Friedman and Suhr. He employs a basic effects setup, usually working with just some delay and overdrive on his guitar tone.

Recommended Listening

Foo Fighters – *Wasting Light*

Foo Fighters – *The Colour and the Shape*

Foo Fighters – *There is Nothing Left to Lose*

Foo Fighters – *Echoes, Silence, Patience and Grace*

This first Dave Grohl riff is based on arpeggios constructed from open position chords. The rhythms are primarily 1/8th notes, but with some tied notes added for rhythmic effect. Try to let the notes of each arpeggio ring for as long as possible and use a light overdrive for the guitar tone with a little added treble boost.

Note that the opening D major chord is played as a Dsus2, but reverts to a regular D major in the final bar.

Example 12a

Single notes feature more prominently in the next example, which includes a syncopated rhythm on bars one and three, where 1/8th notes and 1/4 notes are mixed. Refer to the audio to get the exact rhythm if you need to and, as with the previous example, let the notes ring into each other.

Bar five contains open position chords before returning to single notes once again in the final two bars. Be careful with the 1/4 note triplet in bar seven and allow it to sound for its full duration before playing the octave in the final bar. Try varying the part slightly on the repeat.

Example 12b

Example 12c is constructed from repeated 1/8th notes and is a typical Indie rock rhythm idea. Use all downstrokes for bars one through six to keep an even tone and then use alternate picking in the final two bars.

The two-note figures used throughout reflect the underlying chord changes.

Example 12c

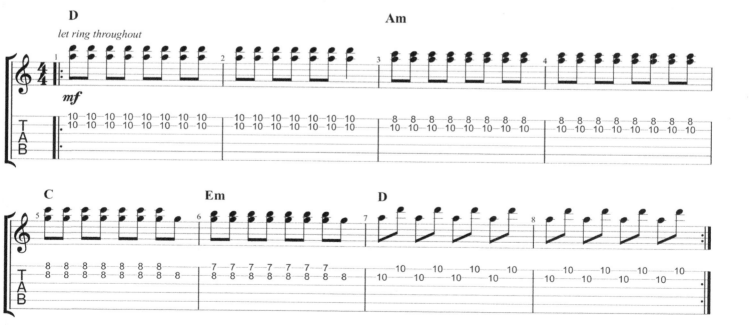

In Example 12d, octaves are used to create contrast from the earlier phrases and you should use a consistent fingering for these. Use either your first and third, or first and fourth fingers. Dampen any un-played strings and pick with a light attack.

In bars six and seven, an Em and D5 chord are introduced before the phrase finishes with a final D octave. The riff is varied slightly on the repeat, so feel free to experiment with your interpretation of the basic part.

Example 12d

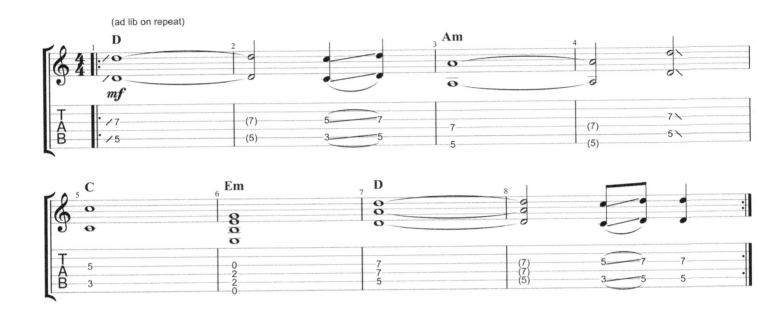

The final riff shows a common melodic device in Indie rock and would work as an instrumental break between vocal lines. The lick is played entirely on the D and G strings and is based around a D7 arpeggio with an added 4th/11th. Hammer-on the note at the 7th fret with your third finger and add a little vibrato on the final note of each bar.

Although the lick is repetitive, it works well against the changing chords of the progression.

Example 12e

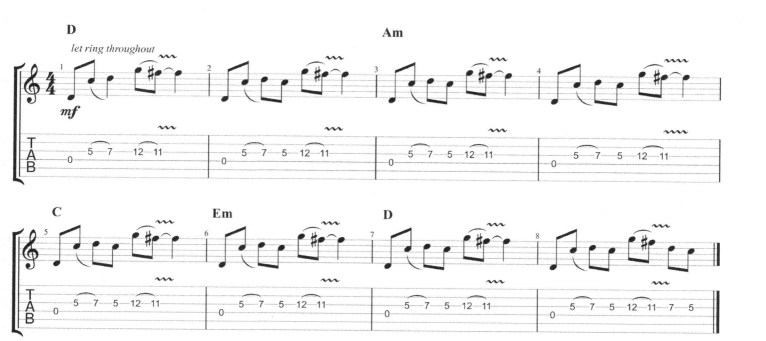

Jack White (The White Stripes)

John Anthony "Jack" White was born John Gillis on July 9, 1975, in Detroit, Michigan. His first instrument was drums before he turned to guitar, influenced by the blues and late 1960s and early 1970s rock. While at high school he met and subsequently married Megan White and took her surname.

When he was 19, White became the drummer for a band in Detroit called Goober and the Peas, until they split in 1996. He worked as an upholsterer by day while playing solo shows and working with local bands at night. In 1997 his wife began playing drums and, with White back playing guitar, they formed a duo named The White Stripes.

The White Stripes released several singles and three studio albums. They came to wider public recognition around 2002 within the garage rock revival scene. Their subsequent albums, *White Blood Cells* and *Elephant* proved commercial successes and the single *Seven Nation Army* had considerable airplay. The duo recorded two further studio albums, *Get Behind Me Satan* (2005) and *Icky Thump* (2007) before they finally broke up in 2011. The couple had not recorded or performed for some time prior to their dissolution and divorced in March 2000.

Since the demise of The White Stripes, White has worked a solo artist, an actor and produced a number of other artists. He also operates Third Man Records which he set up in 2001.

Guitar style, instruments and equipment

White takes a minimalist approach to his guitar playing and his early blues and rock influences can clearly be heard in much of his work. A highly skilled songwriter, he rarely plays indulgent guitar parts, preferring to keep to a "less-is-more" approach like many of his musical idols.

White is a keen user and collector of vintage guitars and uses instruments made by the likes of Harmony, Gretsch and Kay, as well as the more typical Fenders and Gibsons. The choice of guitar depends on the sound and guitar tone he requires for a given project.

For amplifiers he tends to use vintage tube combos, with Fender Twin Reverbs, Bassmans and Vibroverbs being particular favourites. He uses a variety of effects pedals in his live and recording setup including units by Boos, Digitech, Electro-Harmonix and Dunlop.

Recommended Listening

The White Stripes – *Elephant*

The White Stripes – *Icky Thump*

The White Stripes – *Get Behind Me Satan*

The White Stripes – *White Blood Cells*

This first Jack White example alternates between 1/8th notes and 1/4 notes and shouldn't present any major technical challenges. Use a lightly overdriven tone and your bridge pickup to get the sound heard on the recording.

Strive to play each chord with the same volume level and attack, and use all downstrokes with your pick for the entire riff.

Example 13a

This next line is built from arpeggios drawn from common open position chord forms. Make sure you play evenly and in time with the backing track and try to let the strings ring throughout the lick.

The slight dissonance heard between the open G string and the F# note in bars two and four is deliberate and adds a tension to the music.

Example 13b

The next White-style riff owes a little to session guitar players of the 1960s who often played like this on Soul or RnB recordings. The idea is to emphasise the backbeat (beats two and four) of each bar to mirror the snare drum and you should accent these beats as indicated in the notation.

In bars two and four there is also a quick 1/16th note hammer-on played on the final beat to add an extra twist to the part. Use your first and third fingers to play it.

Example 13c

Using only single 1/8th notes, the next riff complements the song's harmony and adds a chromatic passing note between the root notes of each chord. You can see this on the score just before each new chord arrives. Alternate picking will work best here.

Although parts like this sound very simple, it is easy to rush ahead of the beat at this tempo, so make sure you play evenly and consistently.

Example 13d

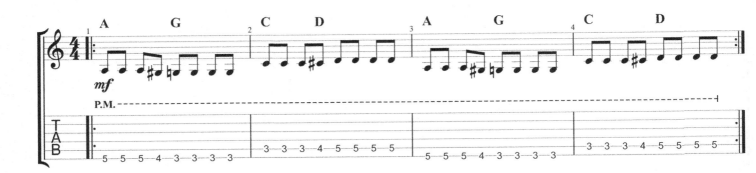

The final idea has a Southern rock feel, principally because of the hammer-on in bars one and three. Use a slightly overdriven tone and make sure you let the strings ring for as long as possible.

The only chords you'll need to play here are the open position G major chord in bars one and three, and the D major chord in bars two and four. This D major chord again uses the G against F# dissonance effect shown in Example 13b.

Example 13e

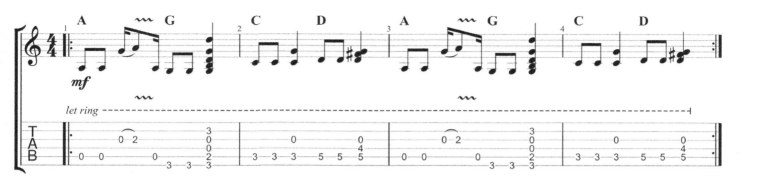

Nick Valensi (The Strokes)

Nicholas Valensi was born on January 16th, 1981, in New York City to a French-American mother and a Tunisian father. He began learning guitar at the age of 5 after picking up one of his father's instruments and reputedly displayed considerable musical talent from a young age. He initially attended The Dwight School and with his interest in music rapidly developing, soon formed a band with two classmates.

Valensi later attended Hunter College where he continued collaborating with other like-minded musicians in various bands until he formed The Strokes with Julian Casablancas, Albert Hammond Jr, Fabrizio Moretti and Nikolai Fraiture in 1998.

The Strokes' 2001 debut album *Is This It* met with considerable acclaim and they were viewed as leading prophets of the garage rock revival scene. Upon the release of their first album they embarked upon a large-scale world tour and in 2002 began working on the follow-up recording *Room on Fire* which was released in 2003. This album went gold, although it didn't achieve the same level of success as their initial recording.

The Strokes have gone on to release a total of five studio albums culminating in the 2013 recording *Comedown Machine*. At the time of writing, Valensi and the group are reportedly working on a new record, although it is uncertain when this will see the light of day. They have continued to perform live since 2013 and in 2017 played a series of festival dates in South America.

Guitar style, instruments and equipment

Valensi's guitar style is bold and authentic, steeped in the tradition of classic rock and roll guitar playing. His influences include Slash, The Velvet Underground, The Cars and Brian May of Queen to name a few.

His principal guitar has been an Epiphone since he began playing them when he was 13, and he uses the company's Sheraton, Riviera and 335 style models. Epiphone have also made him a signature model Riviera with P-94 pickups.

For amplifiers, he favours Fender combos such as the Hot Rod Deville and Super-Sonic, often with Fender cabinets and has also used Sears and Carr amplifiers.

Valensi uses several effects by manufactures such as Electro-Harmonix, Boss, Vox, MXR and Fulltone covering overdrive, delay, reverb and tremolo. Most of his board is set up for different overdrive and distortion configurations.

Recommended Listening

The Strokes – *Is This It*

The Strokes – *Room on Fire*

The Strokes – *First Impressions of Earth*

The Strokes – *Comedown Machine*

Using a simple melodic figure constructed from the E Mixolydian scale, this first riff is played mostly within the 7th position of the fingerboard. Using only the D and G strings, it is simple rhythmically, using just 1/8th notes and 1/4 notes. Play the slide in bar four (starting on the upbeat of the third beat) with your first finger.

In bars seven and eight, pay attention to the change in rhythm to off-beat 1/8th notes. Add a little finger vibrato to the final note.

Example 14a

Guitar parts like the next one can really stand out within a rhythm track. Use a bright guitar tone with a little overdrive. The two-note intervals used here only vary by one note as you move between the B minor and E major chords, with the note on the 10th fret of the B string dropping by one fret to create the new chord.

Example 14b

Another driving 1/8th note part is used in Example 14c, this time using the root of the B minor and E major chords. The entire lick is played around the 4th/5th position and the focus should be on keeping the rhythm consistent. Use a mildly overdriven guitar tone and pick evenly.

Generally, these repetitive 1/8th note guitar parts can be played with alternate picking or with all downstrokes. Experiment to see which sounds best to your ears and more comfortable technically.

Example 14c

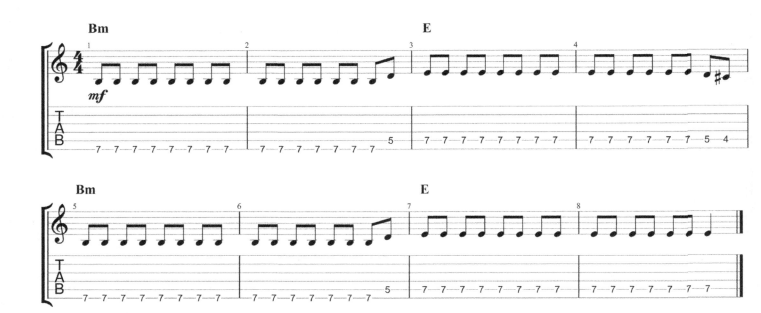

Octaves are the main feature of the next riff. Stick to the same fingering wherever possible and try using your first and fourth (or first and third) fingers to form the shapes. You may have to practise the indicated slides to get them sounding fluent. Try using your neck position pickup for a warmer overall guitar tone.

Example 14d

The final Valensi-style riff continues with the octave approach, but this time played in a higher register. Again, keep to the same fingering for all the octaves and dampen any unwanted strings.

Rhythmically, the whole lick is constructed from 1/8th notes and it shouldn't present any problems provided you keep your timing steady. Just keep an eye out for the offbeat 1/8th notes in the final bar.

Example 14e

Matthew Followill (Kings of Leon)

Cameron Matthew Followill was born on September 10th, 1984, in Oklahoma City. He is best known as the lead guitarist in the US Southern rock group Kings of Leon and the cousin of the three brothers in the band. He began playing guitar at the age of 10 and soon developed great skill on the instrument. This came to the attention of his family who invited him to play when he moved to Nashville in 1999.

Kings of Leon were formed in 1999 and their early music was a mixture of Southern rock and blues-inspired music, until they found a successful and more commercial formula that propelled the group to international recognition, especially in the UK where they had nine top 40 singles and won two BRIT awards in 2008.

The group has recorded seven studio albums beginning with *Youth and Young Manhood* in 2003, and their most recent album *WALLS* was released in 2016. Many of their singles have had major commercial success, most notably *Sex on Fire* and *Use Somebody*, both from the album *Only by the Night*.

By 2016 the group had sold over 21 million albums and 38 million singles worldwide and received 12 Grammy award nominations with 4 wins. The group headlined the British Summer Time concerts in London's Hyde Park in 2017 and remain a very popular touring band.

Guitar style, instruments and equipment

Matthew Followill has a no-frills approach to guitar playing that displays clear influence from Southern rock groups such as Lynyrd Skynyrd and the Black Crowes. He is aware of musical context when creating his guitar parts and generally writes riffs and solos that are tightly knit to the song.

Followill is a devoted player of Epiphone and Gibson guitars, using a Gibson ES-137 on stage much of the time. He also uses a Les Paul Custom, Les Paul Goldtop and a Fender Telecaster.

Somewhat unusually, his preferred amp is an Ampeg Reverb-Rocket, although he also has tried Orange amp heads and a Matchless DC-30 2 x 12 combo. Using a Voodoo Lab Ground Control system live, he operates a collection of different effects which cover delay, overdrive, reverb and pitch shifting. He uses units made by Dunlop, TC Electronic, Line 6 and MXR.

Recommended Listening

Kings of Leon – *Only by the Night*

Kings of Leon – *Because of the Times*

Kings of Leon – *Walls*

Kings of Leon – *Youth and Young Manhood*

This first Matthew Followill-style riff is played using open position chords and requires you to pick small parts of each one, rather than strum the entire thing. Although played mostly in 1/8th notes, there are some tied rhythms to look out for. Refer to the audio example if you need some guidance.

Keep your time steady here and hold down the full chord shapes even though you'll only play small parts of them.

Example 15a

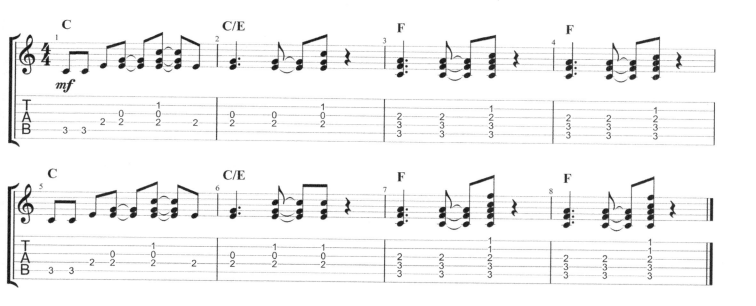

Like many rock guitarists, Matthew Followill often plays steady 1/8th note rhythm guitar parts and this example contains a two-note motif throughout. The notes used here remain constant against the underlying chord changes and the part also utilises a dotted 1/8th note delay, influenced by U2 guitarist The Edge.

If you have a delay pedal or audio plugin that allows dotted delay rhythms, then set it to the tempo of the track to achieve the sound heard on the recording. You will also need to raise the overall delay level a bit higher than normal. Somewhere around 40- 50% wet should work well.

Example 15b

1/16th note rhythms are the foundation of the next idea and you'll need to mute all the indicated notes (those marked with an X). There is a "3 against 4" rhythmic feel to the lick, so listen carefully to the audio to get the exact rhythm. Notice that almost everything is played on the G string.

In bars four and seven, the final note is played with a slight string bend just to add a little variety to the melody. In the final bar there is a hammer-on played in 1/16th notes between the 7th and 9th frets on the G string.

Example 15c

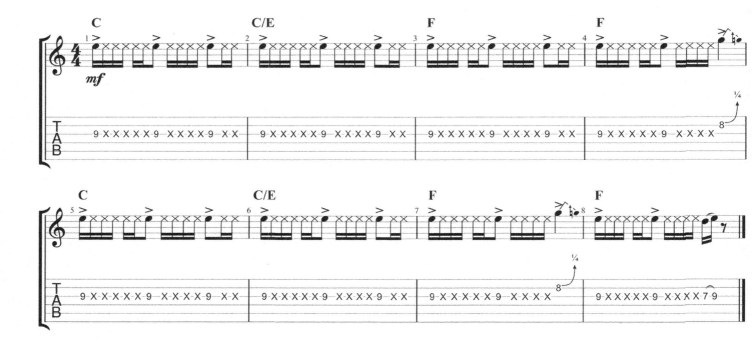

Here's another 1/8th note rhythm guitar idea where the two-note motif changes to accommodate the song's harmony. For consistency of tone, the entire lick is played only on the G and B strings and you will find that using downstrokes throughout will produce the best results.

Guitar parts like this are often more effective in a mix when played with some palm-muting, so use just enough here to make the part sufficiently percussive.

Example 15d

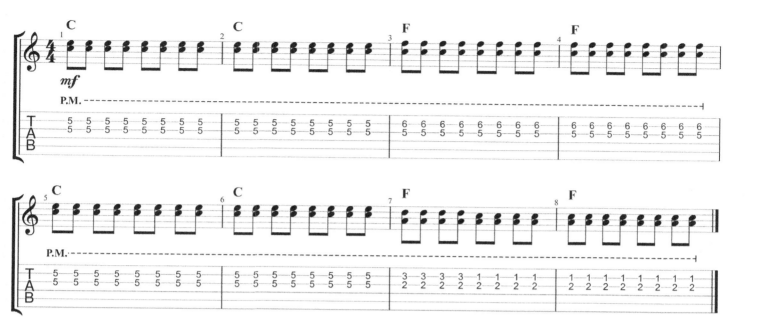

The final riff in the style of Matthew Followill is an example of a counter melody idea that could work well as a short instrumental break, or as support to a vocal line. Mostly composed of 1/8th notes and 1/4 notes, the line contains arpeggio tones from each of the song's chords and demonstrates how a simple melody can be used effectively within a song structure.

Add a little vibrato to the notes sustained over the bar lines.

Example 15e

Andrew White (Kaiser Chiefs)

Andrew "Whitey" White was born on the 28th August, 1974, and raised in Garforth, Leeds, UK. He is best known as the guitarist with the UK indie-rock group Kaiser Chiefs. After completing his A-levels at Garforth Community College in Leeds, and being inspired by new wave and punk music, White met other members of the group while studying at Leeds Metropolitan University.

White's first band was called Runston Parva (named after an East Yorkshire village), but the name was soon shortened to simply Parva. While working at a temporary day job, he was keen to develop the band and with a vibrant music scene in Leeds, the group began to gather a strong following which eventually led to a record deal with the label Mantra.

The group worked steadily for four years until Mantra Records dissolved and the group changed their name to Kaiser Chiefs in 2004. After a brief period of uncertainty regarding their future, the group's fortune changed rapidly with a new record deal and much needed exposure in the music press.

Their debut album *Employment* gained the group significant critical acclaim and commercial success and eventually sold over three million copies. Kaiser Chiefs have recorded six studio albums to date and released several successful singles including the number one hit song *Ruby*. The group has also won three BRIT awards and the NME award for Best Album.

Guitar style, instruments and equipment

Well versed in traditional rock, punk and alternative guitar styles, Andrew White is a seasoned rhythm and lead guitarist with equally strong songwriting and arranging skills, as heard on all his work with the Kaiser Chiefs.

His favoured instruments include a Gibson ES-335, a Gibson Les Paul Standard and a Gretsch Country Gentleman. He has also been known to play a Gibson Les Paul Gold Top.

For amplification he seems to generally use either a Marshall Bluesbreaker 2 x 12 combo (named after the amplifier model Eric Clapton used with John Mayall in the 1960s) or a Vox AC30. He also sometimes uses Orange amps.

His effects are a typical mixture of delays, overdrives and reverbs from manufacturers such as Boss, Ibanez, MXR and Voodoo Labs. He uses Jim Dunlop Tortex picks.

Recommended Listening

Kaiser Chiefs – *Employment*

Kaiser Chiefs – *Yours Truly, Angry Mob*

Kaiser Chiefs – *Off With Their Heads*

Kaiser Chiefs – *The Future is Medieval*

The first Andrew White-style riff is a simple yet effective idea that is used by many Indie rock groups. Strum with a downstroke and sustain each chord for the first three beats of every bar. Play each chord slightly in advance of the downbeat to sound like the audio example.

Use a reasonably bright sound and your bridge pickup for this lick and keep in time with the backing track.

Example 16a

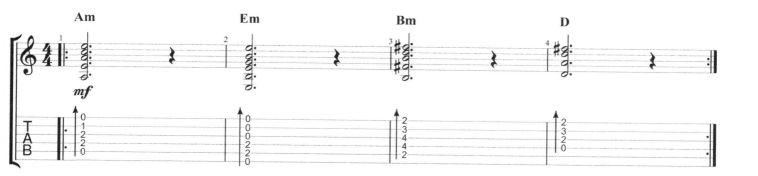

This next riff is played on the backbeat of each bar with 1/8th note rhythmic pairs and triad voicings on the top three strings.

Use a clean guitar tone and play with a crisp pick attack so that the chords are sounded percussively and blend with the backing track.

Example 16b

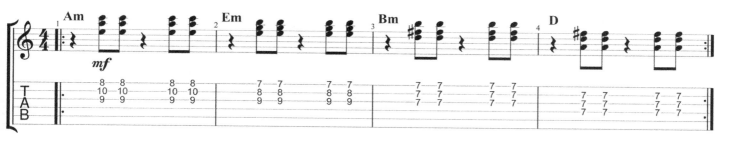

Use a light distortion for the next example and allow the notes of each chord to ring into each other. The entire lick uses common chord voicings and shouldn't present any technical challenges, but you need to ensure that all the 1/8th note arpeggios are played evenly and with the same dynamic.

You might want to try picking every note in this lick or you could try hybrid picking. Either approach will work effectively if you play evenly.

Example 16c

Use prominent reverb and light overdrive for this next White-style riff. It begins with a series of three-note chord structures moving from the A5 in bar to the D major chord in bar four.

The final four bars provide a contrast to the earlier section by using a single note riff over the Am – Em – D chorus section. Moving from chord structures to single notes like this can help create interest with multiple guitar parts and help build energy in the song's chorus.

Example 16d

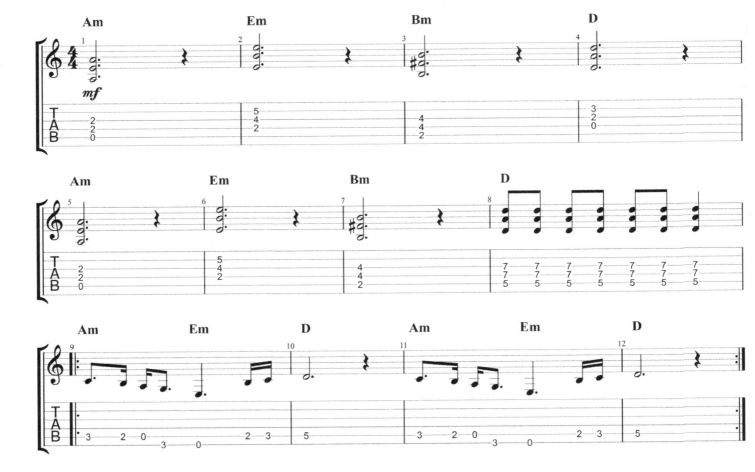

Similar to a classic rock guitar part, the final Andrew White inspired idea uses intervals on the G and B strings for the first three bars. A three-note structure is used for the D major chord in bar four, before the intervals appear again in bar five.

The example concludes with a Hendrix-like rhythm idea played in the 7th position which helps to embellish the basic chord sound.

Example 16e

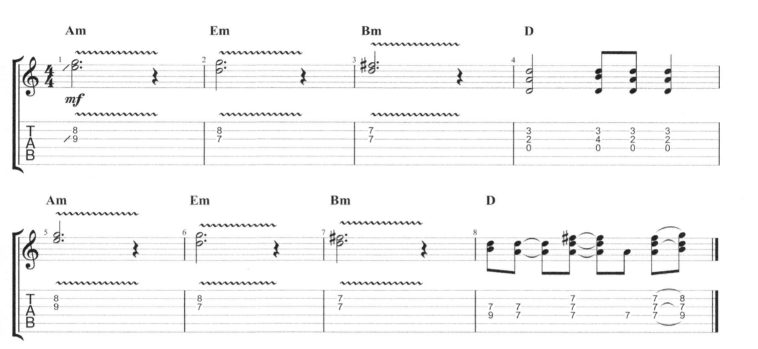

Russell Lissack (Bloc Party)

Russell Lissack was born in Chingford, London, on the 3rd of March, 1981, and is best known as the guitarist in Bloc Party. Lissack attended Bancroft's School in Woodford Green in London and first met future Bloc Party singer Kele Okereke while a pupil there. After attending the Reading Festival together in 1999 they decided to work together and form a band. The group went through a variety of name before settling on the name Bloc Party in 2003 with two additional members, Gordon Moakes and Matt Tong.

Bloc Party, who are principally influenced by rock, also incorporate house music and electronica, and released their debut album *Silent Alarm* in 2005. The album was well received and became the Indie album of the year at the Plug Awards in 2006 and went platinum. A second studio album *A Weekend in the City* was released in 2007 which also charted well. In August of 2008 a third studio recording *Intimacy* was released before the band took time off to focus on other projects.

Bloc Party reunited in September of 2011 to record their fourth album *Four*, which entered the UK charts at number three. Some line-up changes occurred, with two original members leaving and new blood added to the group in the shape of Louise Bartle on drums and Justin Harris on bass. Lissack also formed a new band, Novacub in early 2018 which features Bartle on lead vocals rather than drums. To date, Bloc Party have sold over three million albums worldwide and their fifth album *Hymns* was released in 2016.

Guitar style, instruments and equipment

Russell Lissack's guitar style is influenced by players such as Bernard Butler and Johnny Marr, but very much follows his own direction. He can switch easily between melodic soundscapes to earthy Indie rock stylings and, with an ever-growing effects arsenal, is a keen advocate of distorting and warping natural guitar tones beyond recognition.

He mostly uses Fender Telecasters and owns several models of this iconic guitar. He has also used Epiphone guitars and a Gibson les Paul for some work. He plays Takamine and Fender acoustics.

Lissack favours small tube combo amps and amongst his favourite are Fender's Hot Rod Deville and Blues Deluxe, and Peavey Classic amps. He also uses amps from Audio Kitchen, including their Big Chopper and Little Chopper heads.

A keen user of multiple effects units, Lissack uses pedals from manufactures such as Boss, Electro-Harmonix, Eventide, Strymon and Digitech amongst others. His units cover delay, modulation, reverb, chorusing and pitch shifting. He often combines these to create his signature guitar tones.

Recommended Listening

Bloc Party – *Silent Alarm*

Bloc Party – *A Weekend in the City*

Bloc Party – *Intimacy*

Bloc Party – *Four*

This first, rather hypnotic sounding idea, is constructed entirely of 1/8th notes and should be played with alternate picking for maximum clarity.

The lick itself uses arpeggios of each chord with some extensions such as the 11th on the B minor chord, and the b7 on the E chord. You should be able to play the entire line using your first and third fingers. Use your first finger to bar across both strings when playing notes on adjacent strings.

Example 17a

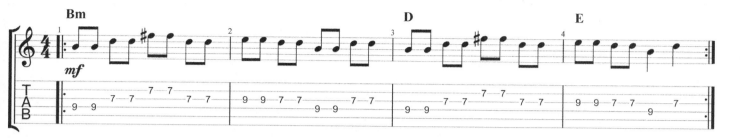

By maintaining a repetitive rhythm, you can quickly create guitar parts that become integral to a song's structure. Using only the root and 5th of the chords, this lick uses the same rhythmic figure in all four bars.

Use a clean or mildly overdriven guitar tone and finger the 5th intervals with your first and third or fourth finger, depending upon what feels the most comfortable.

Example 17b

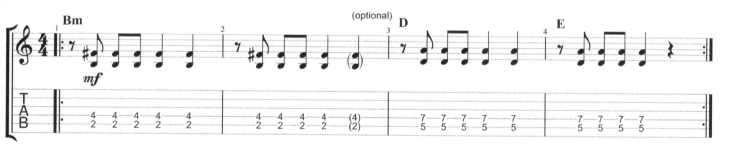

This next riff is comprised of a two-note fragment played in 1/8th notes. There are no great technical challenges here, but make sure you keep your tempo steady throughout. You may want to slightly increase the amount of overdrive you use to match the tone heard on the recording.

Finger the first two bars with your first finger, then use your first and second fingers on bar three.

Example 17c

You can create intensity in a guitar part by using unison bends, such as those in Example 17d. Finger the E string with your first finger and then use your third finger on the B string to bend up to the 12th fret from the 10th.

Try picking the unison bends with a downstroke to keep the tone consistent and cut off the notes before the fourth beat in each bar.

Example 17d

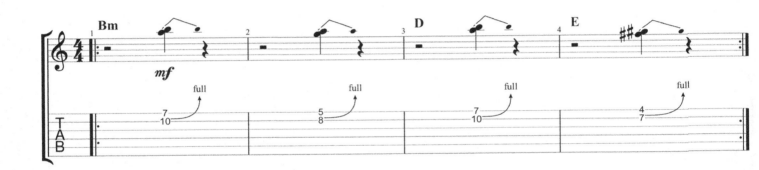

The final Russell Lissack-style riff works well against the swirling synth backing due to its simplicity, and the melody notes should be played with alternate picking for maximum clarity. Try to play each note with even dynamics and add a little overdrive to make the melody stand out against the backing track.

Example 17e

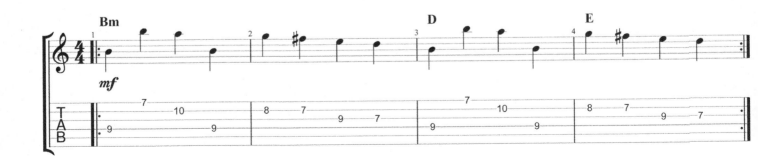

Dave Keuning (The Killers)

Dave Keuning was born on the 28th March, 1976, in Pella, Iowa, and began learning guitar prior to starting High School. At Pella Community High School, he played in the school's jazz band and honed his guitar skills. His influences were artists like the Smashing Pumpkins, David Bowie, Oasis and Radiohead.

Keuning moved to Las Vegas in 2000 where he worked at the Venetian Hotel and The Strip while planning to form an originals band. He placed an advertisement in the Las Vergas Weekly to find like-minded musicians and soon found vocalist Brandon Flowers. The two began writing and were later joined by Mark Stoemer and Ronnie Vannuci Jr.

The Killers evolved from these early writing sessions and the group began working on their debut album *Hot Fuss* which was released in 2004. Their sound was influenced by new wave and post-punk music, and several hit singles emerged from the initial album including *Mr Brightside, Somebody Told Me* and *Smile Like You Mean It*. The album has since gone seven-time platinum.

The Killers have released five studio albums to date, all of which have seen significant commercial success. The most recent was *Wonderful, Wonderful* which was released in 2017. Their tours have seen them play in over 50 countries and they are a major concert attraction. In 2018, Keuning announced that the group were in the early stages of preparing for a new album.

Guitar style, instruments and equipment

Dave Keuning's approach to guitar incorporates unusual chord voicings and occasional dramatic soloing. He is also a skilled arranger and songwriter who contributes significantly to many of the band's songs.

Keuning uses a variety of classic rock guitars including a Gibson ES-335, Fender Stratocasters and Starcasters and Gibson Les Pauls and Flying Vs. For acoustic work, he uses Gibson and Ibanez guitars.

His amplifiers are either Fender or Hiwatt models currently, and he is endorsed by the latter company. His effects (which are wired and operated via an Axess FX1) include boxes by Trex, Boss, MXR, Electro-Harmonix, Keeley and Ibanez and cover chorusing, delay, phasing, reverb and overdrive/distortion effects.

Recommended Listening

The Killers – *Hot Fuss*

The Killers – *Sam's Town*

The Killers – *Day & Age*

The Killers – *Battle Born*

Dave Keuning uses natural harmonics to great effect in his guitar playing. This example requires you to play down the A string in steady 1/16th notes while gently brushing the string with your fingertip to allow the various harmonics to ring out. You can hear this effect in bar two.

After the repeat, there are several standard chord forms of F5, G major and A minor, but note that you don't always play the entire chord shape in every bar. In the final four bars the chords are widened out to include more of the available notes in each shape.

Example 18a

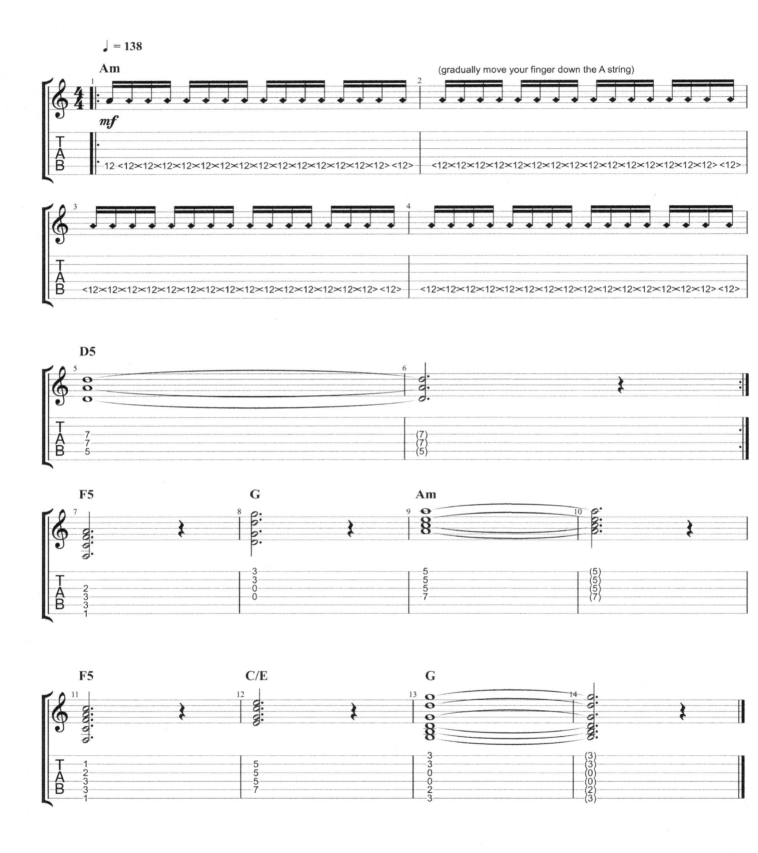

The following riff begins with a steady 1/8th note palm-muted part played on the top two strings. Release the muting for the D5 to open up the sound a little more.

After the 1/8th note interval passages at the beginning of the riff, the second part is chordal with most played on the top three or four strings.

Example 18b

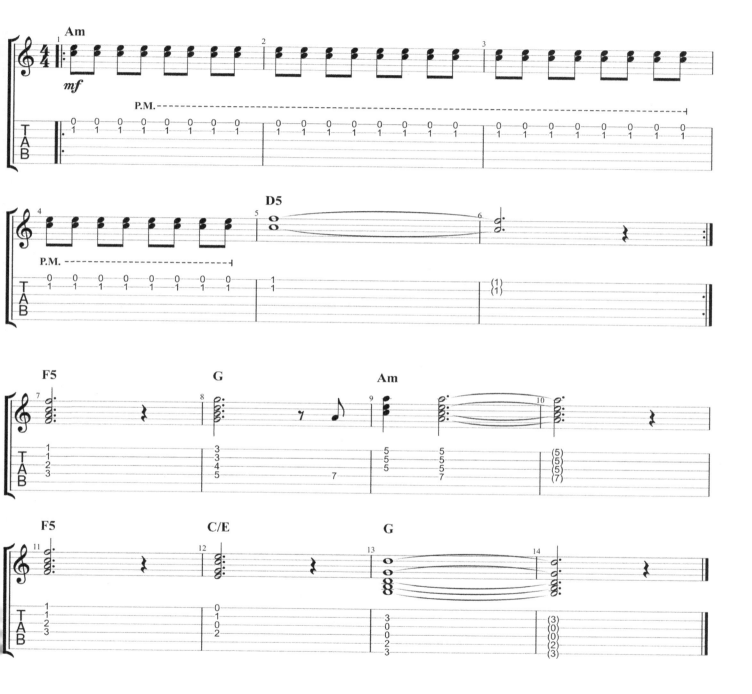

If you use a bright guitar tone and a little overdrive, this next idea will work well in an otherwise busy track. The chords are played on the top four strings and require a barred A minor voicing and an F major triad in first inversion in bar five. (It is used here as a good substitute for the D5 chord in the backing track).

Example 18c

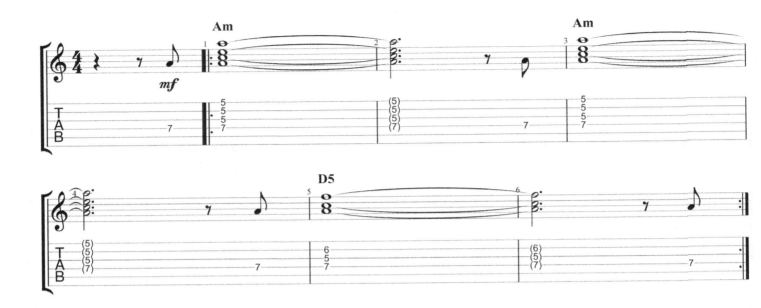

The following riff includes many repeated octave intervals. Ensure you play the slides indicated in the notation on beat one of bars one and three. Try to use a consistent fingering and experiment with either your first and fourth finger, or first and third.

Example 18d

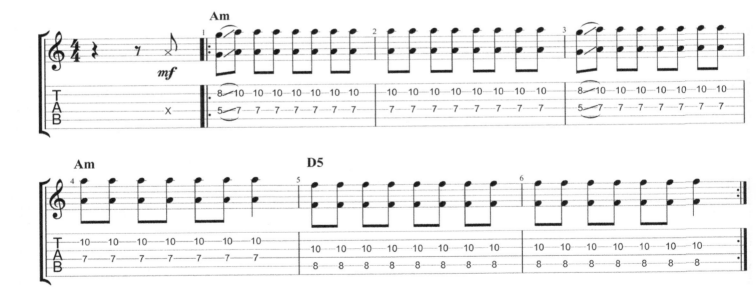

The final riff in this chapter is formed mostly of single root notes played in constant 1/8th notes. Use alternate picking throughout and strive to keep an even rhythm and consistent volume. Many Indie rock guitarists use lines like this to fill out their recording mixes and locking in with the rhythm section is essential.

Example 18e

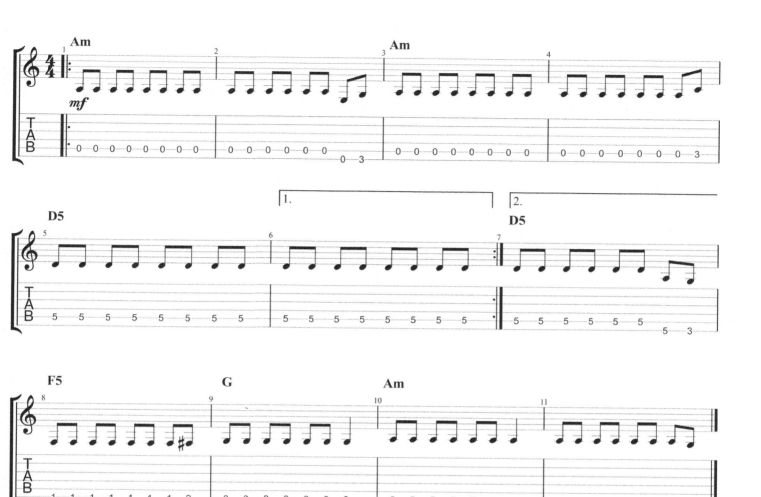

Dan Auerbach (The Black Keys)

Dan Auerbach was born in Ohio on May 14th, 1979, and was raised in the Akron area. He has several relatives who have been involved in music, with his second cousin being the late guitarist Robert Quine. Auerbach grew up primarily listening to blues, although he was influenced by other styles including country and pop.

Best known for his work with the Black Keys, Auerbach first met fellow Black Keys member, drummer Patrick Carney, while they were attending Firestone High School together. Auerbach and Carney began jamming together.

Around this time, Auerbach became infatuated with the blues musician Junior Kimbrough and decided to drop out to concentrate on his guitar playing and songwriting. Auerbach and Carney formed the Black Keys in 2001 and began their career.

The duo eventually signed with the Alive label and their debut album was released in 2002 called *The Big Come Up*. They built a devoted underground fan base and their music became increasingly popular as part of the garage rock revival in the 2010s.

Their breakthrough recording was *Brothers* (2010) which contained the single *Tighten Up* (which won three Grammy awards). Since then the duo have released a further seven studio albums and undertook a world tour in 2014 to support their album *Turn Blue*.

Guitar style, instruments and equipment

Dan Auerbach's guitar style is raw and heavily influenced by the blues musicians he grew up listening to. Taking his blues roots to a new level, his guitar style also incorporates elements of garage and blues rock.

His vintage guitar collection is rather unusual in comparison to some other Indie rock guitarists and includes several lesser known brands. His instruments include a Kent Americana, a Supro Lexington, a Kingston Flying Wedge and a Silvertone 1429 guitar.

Not surprisingly, Auerbach's taste in amplifiers is also vintage in nature, with models such as a Gibson GA-5, Danelectro Commando and a Victoria Double Deluxe combo, alongside the more commonplace Marshalls and Fenders.

His pedals include a wide variety of fuzz and overdrive units coupled with various pitch shifting and delay units. He employs units by Boos, Analogman, Fulltone, Ibanez and Strymon to create his signature guitar tones.

Recommended Listening

The Black Keys – *Rubber Factory*

The Black Keys – *Thickfreakness*

The Black Keys – *El Camino*

The Black Keys – *Brothers*

In the first example, 1/8th note power chords are used for the entire two-chord riff and are a common feature in Dan Auerbach's playing. Play these chords crisply and with an overdriven guitar tone using your bridge pickup. Don't let the chords ring too long to avoid running into the next beat.

Example 19a

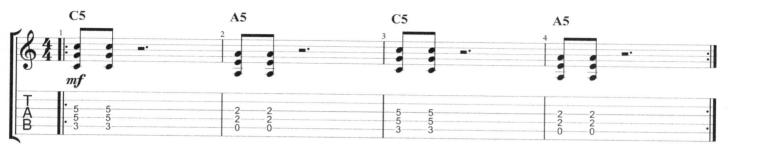

You can hear a lot of rock influences in Dan Auerbach's style and this next example is very much in the blues rock idiom. Using two minor pentatonic fingerboard shapes, the lick begins in the 8th position C minor pentatonic box shape then moves down to the 5th position for the A5 chord.

You can play the lick using just your first and third fingers, but add a little finger vibrato as notated to bring it to life.

Example 19b

This next Auerbach-style example sticks to the backbeat. A little wah-wah is added to really make the lick jump out in the mix. The chords are all played on the top three strings for a brighter sound, and switch between C major and A minor triads.

To add variety to the guitar part, some ghosted strums are added from bar three onwards. Just mute the chord by lifting your fingers up slightly and you will create the effect heard on the recording.

Example 19c

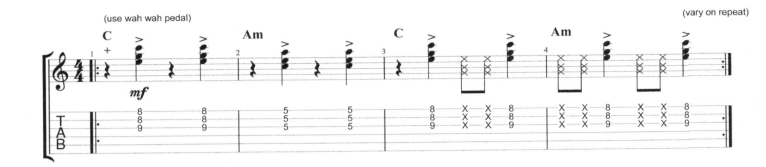

Here's another simple sounding but effective 1/8th note riff played entirely in single notes. No great technical demands here, just solid time keeping and an even tone required. Use a medium overdrive tone on this phrase and either alternate picking or downstrokes.

Example 19d

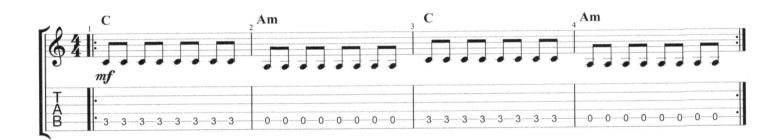

The final Dan Auerbach-style lick just uses distorted barre chords to move between the C major and A minor chords. Don't add too much overdrive or you may lose some definition between the strings. This kind of guitar part is a staple of Indie rock, so play confidently and keep the volume of the chords consistent.

Example 19e

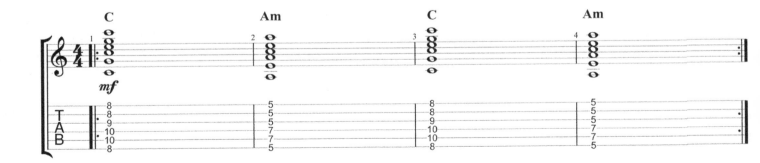

Alex Turner (Artic Monkeys)

Alexander David Turner was born on the 6th January, 1986, and is best known as the front man and songwriter of the UK group the Artic Monkeys. He was raised in the High Green suburb of Sheffield, England. Both his parents worked in education and introduced him to music at an early age. He was given his first guitar when he was 15 and began writing songs using his father's Cubase computer system.

Turner spent two years at Barnsley College studying A-levels in music technology and media studies and, after seeing some of his friends working in local bands, decided to form his own group. In 2002, the band began rehearsing in family-owned garages and played their first gig at a local pub called The Grapes.

The Artic Monkeys began recording demos and soon attracted management who helped them find more gigs and build a reputation as a live band. In 2005 the group came to wider recognition following the release of an EP and their first national tour in the UK. Their first album *Whatever People Say I am, That's What I'm Not*, was released in 2006 and was the fastest selling debut album in UK chart history.

The Artic Monkeys have recorded six studio albums and one live album, and have attracted considerable artistic acclaim. They have headlined Glastonbury Festival twice and won seven Brit awards for Best Group and Best Album.

Guitar style, instruments and equipment

Alex Turner's playing style is typical of the Indie rock and post-punk genres and is influenced by other music such as hip-hop and psychedelic rock.

Turner uses a wide variety of guitars ranging from Gibson ES-335s, through Fender Jazzmasters, Telecasters and Stratocasters. He has also employed ESP, Gretsch and Martin guitars depending on the song he is playing or recording.

His amplifiers are equally diverse, and at various points he has used Selmer Zodiacs, Fender Twin Reverbs, Vox AC30s and Orange amplifiers.

Like many Indie rock players, Turner likes to alter his guitar tones via a variety of effects processers, and his pedals include units made by Boss, Electro-Harmonix, Fulltone, Morley and Ibanez. He also likes to use different overdrives and distortion units for their unique characteristics.

Recommended Listening

Artic Monkeys – *Whatever People Say I Am, That's What I'm Not*

Artic Monkeys – *Favourite Worst Nightmare*

Artic Monkeys – *AM*

Artic Monkeys – *Humbug*

The first Alex Turner-style riff is played on the top four strings for the first three bars and then widens out to an open position E minor chord in bar four. Watch that you correctly play the tied 1/8th note rhythms on beat 2.

This riff is played with a clean Fender-style guitar tone and works with either your bridge or neck pickup equally well. Vary the rhythm a little on the repeat as guitar parts like this aren't normally played identically all the way through a song.

Example 20a

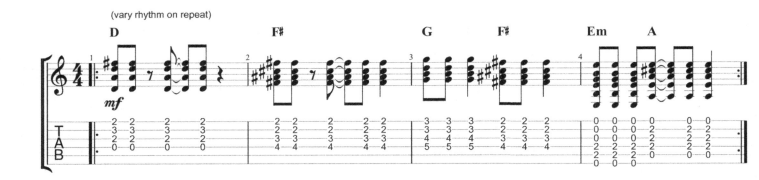

Example 20b looks harder on paper than it is, and uses a mixture of muted strings and staccato chords. It's a good idea to learn this lick in one-bar sections to make sure you play the rhythms correctly and mute the strings where needed.

Use a clean guitar sound with just a small amount of overdrive to thicken up the tone a bit. Keep your strumming hand loose too, as tightening up your pick attack will make it harder to play. Refer to the audio as needed.

Example 20b

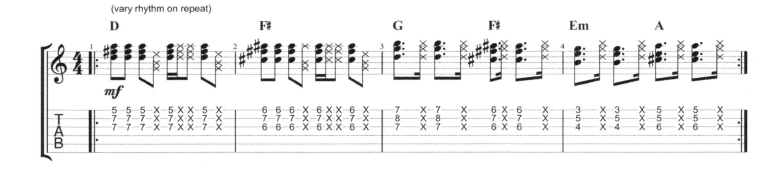

A tremolo effect is added on this next Turner-style riff to add shimmer and depth to the chord voicings. Most are played on the top four strings except for the A major chord in bar four. There's nothing difficult rhythmically in this example, but make sure you play perfectly in time with the backing track.

If you are going to use a tremolo effect with this lick, set it to match the tempo of the song (in this case 122 bpm) to get the sound heard in the audio sample.

Example 20c

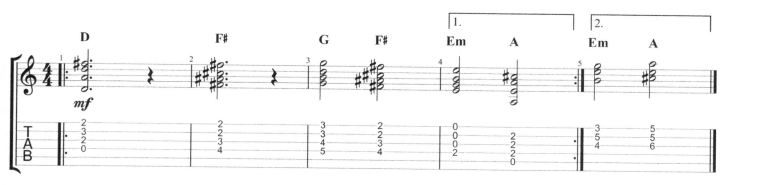

This melody line is typical of Alex Turner's playing style and is played on the G and B strings for a brighter tone. Use your neck pickup and just a little overdrive to thicken the sound. The bracketed notes in bars one, two and three can be played as pull-offs or just picked regularly depending on your preference.

Note how a simple melody like this can work effectively against several chords, and many Indie groups use this approach for short instrumental breaks or to support a vocal line.

Example 20d

The final riff is a low register rhythm part composed of power chord shapes and four-string voicings. Make sure you play accurately on the beats indicated and use just enough overdrive to distort the guitar a little without making it muddy. Use your bridge pickup and play everything with downstrokes.

Example 20e

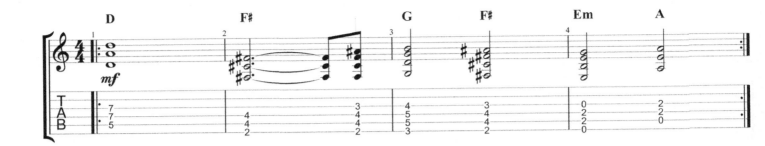

Conclusions

Well, there we have it! 100 awesome riffs in the style of the world's most important Indie rock guitar players. We hope you've enjoyed the journey and that you'll be dipping into this book for years to come.

As we mentioned in the introduction, you'll get the most from this book by making each riff your own. While it's valuable to copy the style of the musicians you love, you'll really benefit from shaping each lick to fit your own voice.

Experiment by changing the rhythm, phrasing, articulation and speed of any phrase to fit your musical personality. That's how language develops and it's how you'll create your own unique voice on the instrument. Just one lick can give you hours of creative pleasure in the practice room.

The best practice you can do is to jam out these ideas with friends. The guitar feels very different when you get away from the comfort of backing tracks.

I'm proud to say that Fundamental Changes has now released over 100 guitar methods and some of those titles will help you develop and personalise your own language in this style.

In particular, I recommend you check out the following titles to help grow your creativity and understanding of the modern guitar style.

The Neo-Soul Guitar Book (with Mark Lettieri of Snarky Puppy) teaches the style that's on the cutting edge of rhythm guitar. There are hundreds of musical examples and full tracks to make you a better, more intricate guitarist.

Indie rock owes a lot of its sound and heritage to classic rock, so my book, *100 Classic Rock Licks for Guitar* will definitely help you build an insight into the repertoire of the musicians that inspired the whole Indie genre.

Finally, developing your technical ability and aural skills on the guitar will make you a more accomplished and well-prepared musician. If you want to link the music you hear in your head to what your fingers actually play, check out *Guitar Fretboard Fluency*. I promise it will make you a better, more creative musician.

Have fun!

Joseph

Other Rock Guitar Books from Fundamental Changes

100 Classic Rock Licks for Guitar

Advanced Arpeggio Soloing for Guitar

Beyond Rhythm Guitar

Complete Technique for Modern Guitar

Exotic Pentatonic Soloing

Guitar – Pentatonic and Blues Scales

Guitar Fretboard Fluency

Heavy Metal Lead Guitar

Heavy Metal Rhythm Guitar

Melodic Rock Soloing for Guitar

Modern Music Theory for Guitarists

Neo-Classical Speed Strategies for Guitar

Progressive Metal Guitar

Rock Guitar Mode Mastery

Rock Guitar Un-CAGED

Rock Rhythm Guitar Playing

Slide Guitar Soloing Techniques

Sweep Picking Speed Strategies for Guitar

The Circle of Fifths for Guitarists

The Complete Technique Theory and Scales Compilation for Guitar

The Heavy Metal Guitar Bible

Ultimate Shred Machine

Made in the USA
Las Vegas, NV
03 March 2023

68479061R00052